A
Travel Guide
to
Heaven

A
Travel Guide
to
Heaven

Anthony DeStefano

IMAGE BOOKS

DOUBLEDAY

New York   London   Toronto   Sydney   Auckland

AN IMAGE BOOK
PUBLISHED BY DOUBLEDAY
a division of Random House, Inc.

IMAGE, DOUBLEDAY, and the portrayal of a deer drinking
from a stream are registered trademarks of Random House, Inc.

Book design by Donna Sinisgalli

The Library of Congress has cataloged the hardcover edition as follows:
DeStefano, Anthony.
A travel guide to heaven / by Anthony DeStefano. — 1st ed.
p. cm.
Includes bibliographical references.
1. Heaven — Christianity. I. Title

BT846.3.D47 2003
236'.24 — dc21
2003043986

ISBN 0-385-50989-8

October 2006

First Edition

1 3 5 7 9 10 8 6 4 2

This book is for
my mother and father

Itinerary

A Special
Preboarding Announcement

All passengers traveling to our final destination today have been awarded a lifetime's worth of frequent flyer miles, entitling them to automatic upgrades to first class. Since the flight is very full, we ask that you check the following items at the gate before boarding: *gloominess, stuffiness, cynicism, pessimism, intellectual snobbery, closed-mindedness, self-righteousness* and *prejudice against God or religion.*

Please be assured you can retrieve this property upon your return — if you wish.

Flight Plan

Down through the centuries, there have been thousands of books written about the subject of heaven. Some have been great theological tomes, some brilliant essays, others beautiful poems. Religious and secular writers from all walks of life have attempted to describe and explain this most elusive of concepts. And yet, while all of these efforts have added to our understanding of heaven, most of them have been missing one key ingredient: fun.

You see, if heaven is anything at all, it's fun.[1] It's a place of unlimited pleasure, unlimited happiness, and unlimited joy. Think about that for a second and consider what an incredibly outrageous concept it is. That's why it's so surprising that while an overwhelming majority of the general public believes in heaven, not many people seem to be bubbling over with excitement about it. In fact, not many people seem to be thinking about it at all.

This is partly because heaven is so hard for us to understand. With all the problems and suffering that constantly envelop our lives, it's difficult to grasp the reality of paradise, a place where there is no pain, no evil, no disappointment, no death.[2]

Another reason is simply that we've heard so much about heaven since our childhoods that the whole idea has gotten a bit stale. Familiarity hasn't exactly bred contempt, but it has bred boredom.

Several years ago, I attended fifteen funerals in seven short months. It was just one of those terribly tragic years that sometimes occur in people's lives. I remember the priests and preachers who presided at these sad affairs trying their best to console all the grieving families and friends. The words they spoke about the afterlife were indeed beautiful and hopeful, but I'm not sure they resonated with all of the mourners who heard them.

This wasn't their fault. They were doing exactly what they were supposed to do—proclaim the Gospel. But unfortunately, for many people the *good news* preached by Christ about the Kingdom of Heaven has become *old news*. Nowadays people seem much more willing to embrace street-corner palm readers and television psychics who conduct séances to summon back the dead. In our eagerness to believe that human relationships continue beyond the grave, many of us have forgotten a very simple truth: all the answers we could ever want about life after death are right under our nose—and have been for two thousand years.

In the case of heaven, the "old news" of traditional Christianity is infinitely more exciting, interesting, uplifting, and fun than anything expounded by TV psychics or "new age" gurus.

Do you know where you can find the best, most accurate descriptions of heaven today? The children's religion section of your local bookstore. Flip through any children's book about heaven and you'll see vibrantly colorful pages filled with rainbows, exotic animals, golden cities, and people playing and laughing. While these books may not explain the sublime and profound mystery of heaven, they are undoubtedly the truest books, because only they convey the unmitigated fun of the place.

C. S. Lewis said that the serious business of heaven is joy. Amid all the boring and esoteric theological discussions, and amid all the confusion of twenty-first-century "pop" spirituality, we sometimes forget this powerful idea. I think it's time we reminded ourselves. And that's why I want to take a different approach in this book.

I love traveling. I love the research, the planning, and

even the packing that go into taking a trip. Ever since I can remember, I've been blessed with the spirit of wanderlust and the love of adventure. For close to two decades, I've had the good fortune of traveling all over the world in my work. One of the things I like best is reading various guidebooks about the places I'm going to visit. These books are not only entertaining, they're also invaluable. After all, when you first go to a foreign country, you don't know exactly what to expect. You've got to be ready to encounter strange customs, strange languages, and even strange people. Even if you don't adequately prepare you might still have a good time, but it certainly helps to have a layout of the terrain and a practical knowledge of the place you're traveling to.

Well, if heaven is anything, it's a *place*.[3] Yes, I know about all the speculation that heaven is really just a "state of mind," and that we should concentrate on "living" heaven "here and now." But that's not what the Bible teaches nor what Christian theologians have taught for two millennia. The one consistent and universal belief about heaven since the beginning of Christianity is that it is a place. A real, honest-to-goodness, physical place.

That's why we don't need another philosophical or theological treatise about heaven. There are plenty of those already. What we need in order to gain an understanding of heaven is not book knowledge, or even deep spiritual insight. What we need is a flair for travel! We've got to be able to take a brand-new look at this very old place. In other words, we need a travel guide. And that's the point of this book.

Some people might object to comparing heaven to a vacation spot, thinking that it trivializes a profoundly important subject. But Christ himself made ample use of travel imagery in the parables he told—indeed, the New Testament is full of people journeying through ancient Palestine, trudging from town to town with their walking sticks, searching for lost sheep, riding along dusty roads on donkeys, and sailing on the Sea of Galilee. All we're doing here is replacing these old modes of travel with some new ones—we're trading in the chariots for jet planes and the fishing boats for cruise ships!

One might expect a book on heaven to be written by a cleric or a professional theologian. I am neither—but that might be just what is needed for our purposes. Sometimes the best way to get a fresh perspective on a subject is to take a few steps back and look at it from the outside. As a dedicated, believing layperson, I believe I'm close enough to provide an accurate presentation of the Christian teaching on heaven, and yet far enough away to avoid bogging you down with too much "formal" theology.

Still, I want to assure you that nothing you are about to read is contrary to either the Bible or the Christian teaching tradition about heaven. While my background is Catholic, I have taken great pains to make this work communicate to all Christians. Of course there's no way to please everyone all the time, and there's bound to be a bit of speculation and imagination in any book about heaven. But that's unavoidable. After all, there's no one around today who's actually been to heaven and back. But you can be sure that nothing in the following pages concerning the basics of heaven is at odds with the major beliefs and teachings commonly accepted by all Christian denominations. Just check the footnoted biblical references in the Scripture Notes at the end of this book and the bibliography to see all the works that have been consulted. I'm not making anything up here. But at the risk of again sounding too lighthearted about such a sublime and serious subject, I'm going to try to inject a bit of fun into the discussion.

And why not? Heaven is dynamic. It's bursting with excitement and action.[4] It's the ultimate playground, created purely for our enjoyment, by someone who knows what enjoyment means, because He invented it. It's Disney World, Hawaii, Paris, Rome, and New York all rolled up into one.

And it's *forever.*[5] Heaven truly is the vacation that never ends.

So for a few hours, forget any hard-to-understand,

preconceived notions you might have about this strange and magical place we've been hearing about since our childhood. Let me take you on a short tour. Fasten your seat belts and get ready for the ride of your life.

And don't bother packing—not even your tooth-brush—because this is one resort that is *really* all-inclusive.

CHAPTER 1

Welcome to Paradise!

When you ask people what they think heaven will be like, most struggle to find a clear answer. Instead of giving you a definite response, they usually grope for various adjectives. These almost always include words like *cloudy, hazy, white,* and *dreamlike*. Sometimes people will tell you they picture heaven as being infused with incredibly intense light. Whatever you imagine heaven to be, chances are that one of the first words that comes to your mind is *spiritual*.

When we do allow ourselves to describe heaven in a material way, we usually think of angels or saints walking around wearing long white robes and choirs singing in the background. The only activity we imagine these strange beings engaging in is never-ending worship of some invisible God, who is as cloudy, nebulous, and undefined as heaven itself.

And then we wonder why no one is excited about traveling to this place!

Well, the first thing to do before we begin our trip is to get the picture of robes and choirs out of our minds altogether. Many of us have such a monumental misconception about heaven that it severely limits our capacity to imagine it, much less look forward to it. The reason is partly that the entertainment industry has programmed us to picture heaven in a very cartoonish way, with clouds, harps, halos, and the like. The real culprits, however, have been poets. Down through the ages, poets have attempted to capture the joy, rapture, and happiness of heaven by giving us an abundance of "ethereal" images. These images, while designed to elevate our souls and show us a glimpse of the transcendent nature of heaven, often have the opposite effect—they leave us flat, dry, and bored.

Now, I am not disparaging poets. They have merely tried to do to heaven what they do to everything else: reduce it to its elemental truth. But in this cynical, skeptical, practical age of ours, we don't necessarily want the elemental truth. We already know that heaven is "paradise" and that we're going to experience "ultimate joy" when we get there. What we desperately want to know is the specifics; we want to know *how* we're going to be so happy there.

Do you want to understand heaven better than you have in your entire life? Do you want to have a true experience of heaven, right this second? You can without reading another chapter. Simply try this experiment: Take the page you're reading and crinkle the corner. Now listen to the sound it makes. Then grab the chair you're sitting on with your hand and squeeze. Feel how hard it is. Then take a deep breath and let your lungs fill with air. Smell the odors of the room you're sitting in. Finally, look around and see all the various shapes and colors of the objects that are before you.

I'll tell you a secret: heaven is going to be like that. Heaven is *physical.*

Don't misunderstand me. That's not all heaven is. Heaven is radically, amazingly, incredibly different from the room you're sitting in. If it weren't, it would hardly be worth the trip. But we have to start with the basics. Before we discuss all the exciting and transcendent spiritual aspects of the place, we need to get straight, once and for all, this fundamental truth: Heaven is, at its core, not only spiritual, but material as well.

If the great monotheistic religions of the world—Judaism, Christianity, and Islam—have taught us anything at all, it's that God is a God of creation.[1] He loves to make things. From the very beginning of the Bible to the very end, God has been busy creating all sorts of wonderful objects: galaxies, stars, planets, oceans, canyons, forests, animals, fish, human beings. You name it, he's created it. And he's always busy using those things to accomplish his will. Very rarely does he snap his fingers and make something appear out of thin air. He usually employs the help of one of his creations to bring about the change or effect he wants. In other words, he usually uses physical means to do the things he wants.

Now, do you really think God is going to abandon his love of creating and his love of the physical, just because this little world of ours comes to an end? Do you think that after all he's done throughout the course of history, he's going to make heaven some cloudy, hazy dreamland? Of course not. That's not the way he operates. Nor is it what the Bible or Christianity teaches.

While Christian theologians have certainly used poetic language to expound upon the spiritual aspects of heaven, for two millennia they have also insisted that heaven will have physical characteristics as well. Indeed, just like the exotic ports of call here on earth, heaven will have its own distinct climate, landscape, and population. Christ himself used very physical images to describe heaven. He said, for example, that in his Father's "house" there are many "mansions," and that he was going there to prepare a "place" for us.[2] In the Book of Revelation, that point is driven home yet again. Even though the biblical description of heaven makes ample use of both literal and symbolic imagery—complete with streets made of gold, pillars made of pearls, and walls adorned with jewels—there can be no doubt that heaven is going to be very tangible. It will be a visible locality, made up of visible structures and materials, with real dimensions and distances.[3]

For some reason, this truth hasn't resonated fully with most people. Yet, it is absolutely essential for all of us to grasp. In fact, if you get nothing else out of this book, understand this one fundamental Christian belief: while heaven is a spiritual reality, it is also very much a place. It is real and it is physical. In some mysterious way, we will be able to touch it, feel it, smell it, hear it, and see it. That means that the life we're going to lead there—despite its transcendent spiritual quality—is going to be much more like the life we're leading now than most of us have ever imagined.

But what about my uncle who passed away last year? What about my grandparents who died when I was little? What about all the good and holy people who have died in the whole history of the world? Are they experiencing heaven as a physical place right now?

The answer to these questions is: no, *not yet*. And before we go any further, it's important to explain why.

There are two fundamental ways of using the word "heaven." When someone we love dies, we often say we hope that person has "gone to heaven." And of course that may be true. Heaven isn't just a place of the future. Heaven exists *now*. Heaven is the word we use to describe the place where God is at this very second.[4] If our friends and relatives who died before us were judged by God as worthy to enter paradise, it's perfectly accurate to say that they are in heaven. As you are reading these very words, your grandmother, your father, your aunt, or anyone else you love who has died may be experiencing the incredible, ecstatic happiness of living with God. But while this is true in the deepest sense, it's also true—as Augustine, Aquinas, and all the great eschatological theologians have said—that they are not yet experiencing heaven to the fullest degree possible.

That's because human beings are comprised of both bodies and souls. When we die, the two are separated—temporarily. Christianity has always taught that on the day of the Last Judgment—at the end of the world—all those who have died will rise, in the same way that Christ did.[5] At that moment, our bodies and souls will be joined again, never to be separated. Before that takes place, however, there will be a period of waiting—a period of time before we get our physical bodies back.

During this interim phase, it won't be possible for us to have *all* the pleasures of heaven. The reason, as we've noted, is that heaven, ultimately, will be physical as well as spiritual—and you need a physical body to fully enjoy a physical environment. You might say that heaven is like a five-star hotel. Just after we die, we can check into a beautiful suite and enjoy many amenities that will make our stay wonderful; but later on—when we're whole again—we'll be invited into the gorgeous penthouse, and be able to experience all the new and exciting sensory pleasures that the entire resort has to offer.

Unfortunately, we have to wait until the resurrection for that "reunion" of body and spirit to take place. How long will that wait be? Only God knows the answer. It may be a few centuries, it may be a few hours. Nor can we venture to guess what that wait will *feel* like to us. Once our souls are separated from our bodies, we will be outside of all time and space. If your mother died fifty years ago, there's no way of knowing if her soul has experienced the passage of time in the same way that you have. Who can say for sure if fifty years of "earth time" will feel like fifty years of "heaven time"? It may not. It may, in fact, seem much shorter. As St. Peter said, with

God, "one day is like a thousand years, and a thousand years like one day."[6]

And yet, there's no doubt that this interim period frightens a lot of people. In fact, it can be downright terrifying if all we imagine death to be is darkness and silence. What we sometimes forget is that we *do* have something to compare the experience to.

Everyone knows what it feels like to be separated from our bodies, because everyone knows what it feels like to dream. Think about this for a moment. When you are sound asleep in bed, your body motionless, you know that in your mind you can be a thousand miles away, sailing on a boat, floating through the air, laughing with your friends, having a perfectly wonderful time. Sometimes, just before you wake up, you may even realize you are dreaming. You may actually be aware that you are in bed and that what you are seeing in your mind's eye is part of a fantasy world.

Regardless of this knowledge, however, the colors you're seeing are just as vibrant, the sounds you're hearing just as clear, the emotions you're feeling are just as genuine. Best of all, the "you" that is living in the dream is really you.

Sometimes these nocturnal musings are so pleasant that we experience a tremendous feeling of disappointment when the alarm clock goes off and rudely calls us back to reality—and to our bodies. We've all felt this let-down at one time or another. The point to keep in mind is that when this happens, we are witnessing firsthand the possibility of experiencing "bodily" sensations without ever moving our limbs or opening our eyes.

Likewise, the period during which our bodies and souls are separated need not be a source of great apprehension to us. The same God who gave us the power to see, hear, and feel things as we sleep will also give us the power to "sense" things as we await the resurrection.

In fact, there's a tremendous amount of real happiness we can have even before we get our bodies back—starting with being with God and with the spirits of our friends and relatives who have died. That's why I know that my saintly grandmother—whose soul I'm confident is in heaven, but whose body has been buried in the ground for four decades—is doing just fine now. I know that she is enjoying incredible company with her dad and mom and siblings, that she can see me and see what's going on in my life, and that she is enjoying all the many gifts, graces, and pleasures that God is bestowing on her spirit.[7]

For the purposes of this book, however, we are not going to speculate too deeply on the exact nature of these kinds of out-of-body joys. Nor are we going to launch into a discussion about subjects that have been sources of serious disagreement between Christian denominations (purgatory, for example). Without downplaying the importance of such doctrinal differences, I want to be clear about this one point: the heaven that we will be traveling to in the pages that follow is our final destination, it is the heaven that we will enjoy after the Last Judgment; the heaven we will experience bodily; the heaven whose existence is universally believed in by *all* Christians; the heaven that you and I will hopefully be permitted to enter one day, at the end of the world.

If that heaven is in your travel plans today, then let's not waste any more time. The flight attendants have closed the cabin doors, and the control tower has cleared us for takeoff.

CHAPTER 2

Luxury Accommodations—
Your New Body

Let's say you wanted to take a special anniversary vacation with your spouse and money was no object. How would you go about planning your trip?

I know that if my wife and I were taking such a trip to, say, Southern California—and I had an absolutely unlimited budget—I'd want a limousine to drive us to the airport and a private Learjet to be there waiting for us on the runway. When we landed in Los Angeles, another limo would take us straight to the Beverly Hills Hotel, where I would treat my wife to a bottle of champagne and maybe some caviar in the Polo Lounge—before checking into the presidential suite.

There, in the luxury of that lush, pink palace, we would enjoy a sumptuous dinner in front of the fireplace, coffee on the shaded veranda overlooking Sunset Boulevard, and perhaps a Jacuzzi in the marble-tiled bathroom before finally retiring to our beautiful canopied bed. And that would be just the start.

Now, I'm not necessarily advocating such delicious decadence on a daily basis, but the question that comes to mind is this: If we would gladly treat ourselves and our families to such first-class service on a simple trip to California, what kind of magnificent accommodations is God going to provide for us when we travel to his own resort—heaven?

And even more importantly, what kind of personal arrangements is God planning for us? What are we going to look like when we get to heaven? What sort of people are we going to be?

If what we've said in the last few pages has sunk in, you probably won't be surprised by the answer. The person that is going to heaven at the end of time is *you*. Not some angel. Not some disembodied spirit. Not some unemotional, spiritual "copy" of yourself that hardly resembles the person you know at all. When you go to heaven after the resurrection, you will be going body *and* soul. You will not be some see-through ghost, floating aimlessly over the clouds.

One of the most crucial concepts to grasp in this book is that your body is not something that simply houses your spirit. So many people have a mistaken notion about this. They think that because our bodies deteriorate and die, and because our spirits are "eternal," that somehow the two are not really connected, or that the spirit is better than the body.

Not so. We're supposed to be living in a "material age." And yet, when people think about heaven, they forget all about "matter." It is one of the true ironies of life that the people you would least expect—the Church leaders and theologians—are the ones who have turned out to be the real champions of the material world. For in the long history of Christianity, few heresies have been slapped down harder or faster than the ones that proclaim the superiority of the spirit. Gnosticism, Manicheanism, and a host of other "isms," as well as the majority of Eastern religions, have all tried to claim that the soul is "good" and the flesh "bad": that once we die, we will finally be liberated from this troublesome shell we call a body and will be free to be happy.

That's not the approach of *any* of the Christian churches. We believe that God didn't just create a spirit and dress it up in a body. We believe He created bodies and souls together and that they make up one single entity that we call a human being. In fact, the very term, "human being," illustrates the material and spiritual makeup of our identity. It is this complete identity that is destined to live in heaven, not just the human spirit.

That's why it's so important to pay our respects to deceased friends and relatives at the cemetery. Sometimes you hear people say that they don't think that's necessary because the person's "not really there," that he or she is "with God," or that the best thing to do is "say a prayer" for the person's soul.

The problem with this kind of thinking is that it's only half true. As we've said, after someone dies, only part of the person is with God. The other part—the person's body—is still here with us on Earth. When we visit someone at the cemetery, we are showing that we understand and believe this truth: that the person we loved is not just a spirit, that he or she is going to be a whole person once again. Justin Martyr, writing a little more than one hundred years after Christ's own bodily resurrection, summed it up perfectly: "If God has called humans to life and resurrection, he has called not a part, but a whole—and that is the soul and the body."

The question is: What are we going to be like once we are "whole" again in heaven? Common sense tells us that if God went through the trouble of making us, he's not going to simply throw us away. He's going to change us, certainly. We won't be exactly the same in heaven as we are right now. In fact, as we're going to discuss, these changes will be both dramatic and exciting; and they are going to make our life in heaven a lot more fun. But in another very real way, our resurrected bodies will be strikingly similar to what we have now.[1] Let's focus on that for just a moment.

To start with, our bodies are going to be made up of atoms and molecules and cells. How do we know that? Because that's what a "body" is. That's what makes it different from a spirit; it's not a spirit because it has mass and weight and form. Tertullian, another famous Christian theologian, wrote about this in A.D. 210, saying that our bodies will rise again and that they will be "certainly the same flesh, and certainly in its entirety." Thus, in heaven, the body is going to have a skeleton, just as we have now. It will have a circulatory system and blood coursing through its veins. It will have skin, which will feel warm to the touch. It will have a respiratory system, a digestive system, and a nervous system. In every way you can imagine, it will be a real, authentic, physiologically accurate human body.

And it will be the body of either a male or a female. If you're a man now, you're going to be a man in heaven. If you're a woman, you're going to be a woman in heaven. This may seem like a straightforward point, but you'd be surprised how many people question whether or not heaven is made up of strange androgynous creatures. How boring would heaven be if that were true?

Because we'll have human bodies in heaven, we'll also be able to do all the things we do right now. We'll be able to use our senses, for example. We'll be able to eat in heaven, drink in heaven, and talk in heaven. We'll be able to see, hear, run, and whistle a tune. People in heaven will be able to sit in a chair and read a book like you're doing right now. They'll be able to hug and kiss one another. They'll be able to snap their fingers, brush their hair, take a long walk, or create a work of art with their hands.

We are going to talk a lot more about the kinds of activities that go on in heaven later on, but for now, understand this one point: the good Lord gave us bodies that are capable of doing all sorts of interesting and incredible things. As long as we have those bodies, we're going to have the ability to do those things. Our bodies won't just stop acting like human bodies just because they're in heaven.

They also won't stop being *our* bodies. In other words, we'll be able to recognize each other in heaven as the people we knew on earth.[2] I'm not going to stop being Anthony DeStefano when I get to heaven. I'm going to have my body, my mind, my memories, my personality, my consciousness. I'm going to be *me*. Whatever makes me the person I am is what I'm going to keep in heaven.

The point is that people don't lose their identity when they go to heaven. And that includes their physical identity. If you have brown eyes now, you're taking those brown eyes with you to heaven. If you're a redhead now, you'll be a redhead in heaven. If you are white, black, or yellow now, you'll have that coloring in heaven. If you have a mole on your left cheek now, you'll have one on your left cheek in heaven too.

In other words, if you want to know what you're going to look like in heaven, go take a look in the mirror right now!

But what if I hate the way I look now, you say? What if there are things about my body that I want to change—that I need to change—if I am going to be perfectly happy in heaven? Do you mean I have to stay the way I am now for all eternity? Absolutely not.

You have to trust God just a little bit. He knows better than you what is wrong with your body and how it should be fixed so that you will be happiest in heaven. "Do not be anxious," Christ said. "If God so clothes the grass of the field, which is alive today and tomorrow is thrown into the oven, will he not much more clothe you? Oh men of little faith!"[3]

And Augustine, one of the greatest Christian theologians in history, called God a wonderful "artisan," who would undoubtedly restore our bodies back to life and "take care that nothing unseemly result."

Just because you're going to keep your identity in heaven doesn't mean you're going to be exactly the same. There are going to be outrageous differences that only God could think up. The key word in this whole discussion is *identity*. Who are you, really: physically, psychologically, and emotionally?

In order to help you to improve your life, motivational speakers and personal development experts often tell you to start by making a list of the characteristics and qualities you identify with yourself. This is a great exercise because it forces us to define how we perceive ourselves. When we complete the list, we usually find that there are many characteristics we are pleased with—"I'm outgoing, generous, adventurous, pretty," for example—and many that we wish we could change—"I'm lazy, fat, angry, depressed, undisciplined," etcetera.

Well, do you really believe that you are *equal to* those "negative" characteristics that you listed? Is that who you are, at your core? Is that your identity?

In most cases, the answer is no. You might indeed be lazy, overweight, angry, depressed, and undisciplined, but those traits don't define your essence as a human being.

They are imperfect qualities that you have acquired over time because of a genetic predisposition, from your environment, or through your bad choices and habits.

Because they are not part of your real identity, they have no place in heaven. Therefore, they are not making the trip with you. You can say good-bye and good riddance to them once you leave this life.

On the other hand, what about the *real* you? Can we even know what that is?

Have you ever had a day in your life when everything was going right, when you could do no wrong? Try to seriously recall a time when you were at your absolute peak, when you were acting, thinking, and feeling your best. A day when you were entirely energized, enthusiastic, and passionate. A day when you were at your maximum level of performance, psychologically and emotionally. When you were bold instead of timid, strong instead of weak, confident instead of fearful. In other words, have you ever had a day when you were truly being the kind of person you know you have the power to be?

Everyone has experienced a few days like these. Most of us don't have them as often as we wish. In fact, very few of us live up to our full potential all of the time. The few special individuals who do stand out from the crowd. They're the ones who are literally radiating energy and charisma. They're the people who are most enthusiastic and most passionate about living, regardless of their station in life. But though we don't always actualize our potential, we do occasionally "hit our stride," so to speak, and are able to show the world and ourselves what we are really made of.

It is at those times that we are able to see our true identity. That's the identity that God always sees in us; it's what he had in mind when he created us.

That's what we will be like in heaven.

The same goes for our physiology. If you are sixty-two years old and are reading this book now, I don't have to tell you that your identity is not "sixty-two." On the inside, you know you're still twenty-five! Time might have unfairly rocketed you to your present age, and your body might have suffered in the process, but that doesn't change the fact that at your essence, you are still the same person you were forty years ago.

And if you're two hundred pounds overweight, I don't have to tell you that it is not your identity to be obese. Nor is it your identity to be crippled or deformed or diseased. Nor blind or deaf. None of those things make up your core person. The simple point is that when you enter heaven, you will enter as your truest self, your *best being*—emotionally, psychologically, intellectually, and physically. Whatever that is, and only God knows for sure, is what you're going to be like in heaven. In some cases, we're going to see people in heaven who look exactly as they did on Earth; in some cases they'll be younger, in some cases older (if they died as infants or unborn babies), in some cases thinner.

No matter what the changes, though, one thing is certain: we will positively be able to identify the people we knew and loved in life. How will you recognize your grandfather who died at eighty-seven if in heaven he looks as young and vibrant as he was at thirty? Well, he might just have to introduce himself to you at first! You may need a little time getting used to seeing him as a young man. Or, God may simply give you the ability to immediately see him for who he is. No one can say for sure how God will work all his miracles, but there is no question that we *will* recognize our father as our father, our grandmother as our grandmother, our children as our children.

And that's not even the best part. God has other exciting changes in store for us as well. In fact, he's gone out of his way to tell us exactly what those changes are and demonstrate them to us with a living, breathing example. How so?

We see at the end of all the Gospel accounts a stunning description of what Christ was like after his bodily resurrection. Even if you're not a Christian, it's fascinating to read what the Bible says about this, because it provides us with a glimpse of how we are going to act, live, and be in heaven. The passages I'm referring to center around the various appearances Christ makes to his disciples after he is crucified and then rises from the dead on Easter Sunday morning.[4] It's almost eerie to see how Christ is suddenly present in a room one moment, and then disappears into thin air; how he is able to move silently through walls, and ascend into the sky; how he has the power to let himself be recognized or not by the people around him. At the very same time that he is showing his power over physical laws and the material universe, he is eating fish with his disciples, having conversations with them, and making them touch his body to show them that he is real, and not a phantom.

What God has done in these short paragraphs is pull back the veil of secrecy that shrouds heaven, and reveal, for just a brief moment, what life there is going to be like. As St. Paul said when describing our life in the world to come, Christ will "change our lowly body to be like his glorified body."[5]

Theologians have analyzed the postresurrection appearances of Christ and drawn many implications and conclusions about the nature of the risen body. Thomas Aquinas, the great Catholic saint and philosopher of the thirteenth century, listed four distinct qualities that our bodies will have in heaven, qualities that mirror what Christ displayed in the Bible: subtlety, luminosity, agility, and incorruptibility.

What it all comes down to is a basic transformation of how your body operates. Right now, your physiology is very much in control of how you act and what you do. If you're hungry, for example, you eat, if you're thirsty you drink, if you're tired you sleep. You can fight against your body, of course, but eventually, you have to lose. Everyone has heard the expression: "The spirit is willing, but the flesh is weak."[6]

That's exactly what I mean.

In a million different ways, we are slaves to our bodies, some individuals more so than others. When we see people who have no ability to discipline their physical desires, we say they have no "self-control," or "willpower." Sometimes this inability can wreak havoc in our lives. For example, we know we shouldn't eat all that ice cream and fast food, but we just can't resist, so we end up with heart disease. We know we should exercise every day, but our bodies are just too tired from the pressures of work, so we watch TV instead, and wind up with extra pounds and no energy. We know we should be faithful to our spouse, but we just can't control our sex drive, so we start a mindless affair that eventually leads to divorce.

So many lives, so many families, so many marriages

have been destroyed because our "will" is subservient to our bodily cravings.

Fortunately, when we get to heaven, a startling reversal takes place. Our *bodies* suddenly become totally subservient to our *wills*. What that means is that, in heaven, we will no longer be plagued by any of the unhealthy, unethical, unintelligent compulsions that drive our behavior right now. We won't have any vices, bad habits, or urges we can't control. We'll finally be in total command of our actions and behavior. At last we'll be able to live at our full potential.[7]

The same will be true for us physically. No longer will we be at the mercy of our cravings. Thus, when we eat in heaven—and there is no reason to believe we won't—it will be to enjoy the pleasure of the taste of food, not because we have to absorb nutrients to survive.

The really exciting thing, though, is that when God says our bodies will be at the absolute service of our wills, he means *absolute*. When Christ appeared to his disciples in one place, and then suddenly vanished and appeared to some other disciples in another place many miles away, he was demonstrating that he had absolute control over where and how his body traveled. The implications for us are staggering.

Imagine for a second that you have 100 percent control over your body. Imagine you can tell it to do anything you like, and it will listen. It goes without saying that you can control hunger, thirst, tiredness, etcetera. But think bigger than that. Try thinking like God!

Right now, for instance, I'm sitting at a computer in my office. After I'm finished writing, I would love to be in Rome, sitting in an open-air café on the Via Veneto. Or maybe skiing in the Swiss Alps. Or maybe taking a leisurely stroll down the Champs Elysées in Paris. Or, who knows, maybe even playing golf on the moon.

Obviously this is just idle daydreaming. But in heaven, it will be reality. In heaven, the body is going to have the power to listen to those kinds of commands. It will do whatever we tell it to do, and go wherever we tell it to go, instantaneously. I know that might seem too incredible to believe, but that's what Christianity has taught for two thousand years. It's just that people don't always bother to think about the specific conclusions that flow from what they already believe.

Another amazing thing is that your body will be *indestructible*. Because it will be controlled by your will, it won't be susceptible to pain or suffering.[8] If you really want to understand what this means and are not afraid of feeling a little silly, pick up a comic book and read about the various superheroes with their incredible superpowers. These invincible, make-believe men and women provide as good an example as any theology textbook can give of the powers we will have in heaven.

And why should that be such a surprise? When human beings try to imagine the kind of powers a superhero might have, they naturally invent someone with the ability to defy the physical forces of the universe. That's exactly what the Bible and the Christian tradition say about our life in heaven. We're not that far off in our thinking. We just have to resist the inclination to dismiss the idea just because it seems funny and outrageous. We have to get used to the idea that God himself is outrageous. If we, with our little, limited imaginations, can conceive of a Superman, don't you think God can come up with something at least as good?

All of this should give you at least some idea of what we're going to look like and be like in heaven. Perhaps you're already starting to realize that there are some pretty interesting possibilities in terms of what we are going to be able to do once we obtain these "new and improved" bodies. But let's not jump ahead. Before we discuss the activities we're going to enjoy in the afterlife, we need to explore the terrain a little.

What, exactly, are the "sights to see" on this eternal vacation? Let's think about what this strange place actually looks like.

CHAPTER 3

Our Final Destination

Anyone who spends a lot of time on trains and planes is familiar with the term "final destination." Often we're impatient when it comes to traveling because we don't want to make any stops en route. After all, is there anyone who really enjoys layovers or connecting flights? Most of us want to get to where we're going instantaneously, just like the characters on *Star Trek* who simply "beam over" whenever they have a trip to make.

Ironically, the opposite is true when it comes to our *real* final destination—heaven. Most of us want to make a million stops before we get to that place! Part of the reason is that we're afraid of the unknown. If we had a good picture in our minds of what that destination looked like,

35

maybe we wouldn't have to be dragged kicking and screaming when God calls us home.

The good news is that we have such a picture! As a matter of fact, we've had it for two thousand years. It's right there in Scripture and Christian theology. All we have to do is take the time to make some basic theological deductions and perhaps use a little of our God-given imagination.

Did you ever see *The Wizard of Oz*? Remember how Dorothy and her three friends go off in search of the things they each want most in the whole world? Things they feel they either lost or never had to begin with? One wants courage, one intelligence, one a heart, and one a true home. The moral of that story is that you really don't have to embark on a long journey to a see a wizard in order to secure those things. In fact, if you really want to find them, you probably don't have to look farther than your own backyard.

Heaven is a little like that. People think of it as something so far off, so unclear and hazy, that they can't focus on it. They don't realize that what they're looking for is right under their nose.

We said in the last chapter that if you truly want to see what you're going to look like in heaven, you should take a glance in the mirror. Guess what? If you want an idea of what heaven is going to look like, go take a walk around the block. If you want to know where it is, don't strain your eyes looking high up into the sky. It's not beyond the stars or over any rainbow. It's right here, under our feet.

The physical location of heaven is *Earth*.

In the New Testament, there is much talk of a "new heaven and a new earth."[1] What this simply means is that in the same way human beings are destined to experience death, bodily resurrection, and transformation, so too will our own planet.

We've already said that when you arrive in heaven, you're going to be very similar to, but also a lot different from, the way you were in life. You're going to have the same identity, and will be totally recognizable as *you*, but you'll also undergo some pretty fabulous changes that will enable you to enjoy heaven to the fullest.

The same is going to hold true for Earth. God's going to use the same pattern and the same model that he uses for us. You see, if God is anything, he's consistent. If he's already shown us that he intends to make use of the "raw material" of human beings in heaven, then you can be sure he's going to continue to use the raw material of the world around us. Why would he go through the trouble of making the Earth in the first place if his only intention was to throw it in the incinerator later on? God's not going to waste anything he's spent so much time and effort creating.

In the very first book of the Bible, Genesis, God created the Earth and saw that "it was good." Well, do you think he is in the habit of discarding the good things he invents? Of course not. In science you may have heard of the "Law of Conservation of Matter," and the "Law of Conservation of Energy." Well, God's got a law too. It's called the Law of Conservation of Creation. He doesn't create good, imaginative things, "work" on them for millions of years, and then toss them to the side like a toy he's bored with. He may change and transform the things he creates, but he doesn't eliminate them—at least not permanently.

To put it simply, our final destination as humans is not some unidentified point of light zillions of miles from where we are now. Nor is it some psychological state of mind. Our final destination, ironically, is right here on good old planet Earth. The Bible makes it crystal clear that, at the very least, *part* of heaven will be this "new Earth." And it will be the same earth we've lived on during our lifetimes, the same Earth that has been the home to billions of human beings over the long course of history. But like human beings, the Earth itself is going to experience a death and resurrection of sorts.

Scripture teaches us that the world we are living in

now will come to an end one day. It will "die" just as human beings must die. We call that event the Apocalypse. But afterwards—after the destruction of the "old" world—there is going to be a "new" one. The Earth we live on now is going to undergo a stunning, spectacular transformation. This new, transformed Earth will form part of what we call heaven.

Now what, exactly, will this place look like?

Before we start going into details, let's take a moment to review our methodology. I said earlier that everything you read in this book is totally consistent with both the teaching of the Bible and with Christian theology. And that's the truth. But does that mean that you are going to find anything in the Bible or the writings of the saints that compares your resurrected body to Superman? Not very likely. What we do have, however, are four Gospel accounts that relate how Christ looked after he rose from the dead. We have Paul's first letter to the Corinthians, in which he teaches that Christ represents the first fruits of what is to come.[2] And we have scores of letters, books, and sermons from the Church fathers and from hundreds of other theologians and martyrs who have prayerfully analyzed these passages and have assured us that the risen Christ is the pattern God will use to re-create humans after we rise. All that I have done by using the Superman analogy is put two and two together.

What I intend to do throughout this book is take well-known, commonly accepted, rock-solid Christian teachings, and draw out the exciting implications. My approach here is not to invent new things about heaven, but rather, to be a kind of theological Sherlock Holmes. We have two thousand years of biblically based teachings on the subject of heaven. We need to start making some simple deductions about what those teachings mean for *us*. It's really very elementary.

We know, for example, that God is going to transform the Earth we live on and make it "new," that he's going to keep it very much the same, but also make it somehow different. We also know that this new Earth won't be just spiritual in nature, but rather, physical and material. Finally, we know it's going to be a place of ultimate joy and pleasure for us. All this we know from theology. We also know from our own experience of living in the world that God has a great imagination. That he loves to make things—interesting, wild, colorful, outrageous, surprising things.

Based on all this, it's not very hard to come up with some simple but accurate ideas about what heaven is going to look like. For example, let's start with a few *visual* deductions.

Is there the slightest doubt, knowing what we know about God and how he operates, that heaven is going to be lit up in bright, vivid Technicolor? Can anyone seriously believe that heaven is going to be all cloudy and white, like we see it portrayed in the movies? If anything, Technicolor is the *least* that heaven is going to be. On Earth, humans are able to see only the basic colors that make up the light spectrum: red, yellow, blue, and white. All the other colors we know are just combinations of these four.

In heaven we'll certainly see these basic colors, but we'll also see new ones that we've never even imagined. In fact, God's given us a great clue that these new kinds of colors can exist, because he's gone ahead and created a few already. You've heard of ultraviolet and infrared light? These colors exist, but our eyes are not able to see them. I'm willing to wager they'll be visible to us in heaven.

And that's just the beginning. Everything we know about God tells us that heaven will be literally bursting with color. Think of the most colorful sunset you can imagine. Think of the reds, yellows, oranges, pinks, and blues. Think of the thrilling effect a sunset like that can have on your spirit. Now realize that only four basic colors go into making that beautiful picture. Let me ask you a question: do you think God has only four colors on his palette?

In heaven, the main purpose of God's creations will be to give us unbridled joy. There's a famous quote from the Bible that says: "Eye has not seen, nor ear heard, what God has prepared for those who love him."[3] We have to take that statement very literally. Heaven is going to be a feast for the senses.

And this feast will by no means be restricted to the sense of sight.

Do you think you've tasted some good food in your life? Well, wait until you taste the food in heaven! Not only will you be able to eat the familiar foods you had on Earth, but there will be new ones to try—with brand-new flavors and brand-new tastes.

Do you think you've heard some pleasing sounds in your life? Is there a particular kind of music that always puts you in a good mood or makes you feel incredibly happy? Well, heaven is going to have music too, and I guarantee you it won't be just choirs singing and harps playing. There will be orchestras and bands and singers and instruments. You will be able to experience all the kinds of music you know and love now, and new, unimaginable kinds as well.

The same thing goes for our sense of smell and touch. In heaven there will be new scents and odors to enjoy, and new textures and shapes to feel. If we want to understand heaven, we have to try thinking like God! And that means we have to free our imaginations and get a little outrageous.

In fact, let's take that thought one step further. In grade school we were all taught about the four basic categories of nature: fire, water, earth, and air. Later on, we learned how these categories could be broken down even further into the periodic table of elements. Everything we know—the oceans, the sky, the mountains, the grass, the cities, the living creatures—is somehow a combination of these elements. But in heaven, why would God limit himself to only what is on that chart? Will God really be satisfied with such a finite number in heaven—his superplayground for the human beings he loves so much?

I don't think so. Just as there will be new sights, sounds, and sensations in heaven, so too will there be new basic elements. And from these basic elements, whole new categories of nature will come about. Now, I have no idea what these marvelous categories might be, but knowing God, they'll be as vast and awe inspiring as the ocean and sky.

It all comes back to what we said in the last chapter about the real "materialists" in life being the Church leaders and theologians, because they, more than anyone else in history, have recognized the true value of material things in God's plan. What we're emphatically saying in these pages is that God himself is a materialist of sorts. Even more, God is a *sensualist*.

The heaven that the Book of Revelation speaks of,

the heaven that Augustine writes about, the heaven that Christianity proclaims today, is a sensualist's delight. God must have quite a laugh when atheists and agnostics here on Earth talk about religion being "gloomy" and "sad," and ridicule those who believe in God as being "against sensual pleasures." Nonsense! We understand how important and exciting those sensual pleasures are much more profoundly than atheists ever will, because we know those pleasures are going to be brought to even greater intensity once we get to heaven.

Of course this doesn't mean that *all* material and sensual pleasures are going to be experienced in the afterlife. We know very well that many earthly pleasures—because they have been distorted by human selfishness—can be classified as sinful and ungodly. Obviously these won't have any legitimacy in the heavenly realm. But there are so many others that *will* carry over to eternity.

Let's use the example of nature. Do you think that in heaven there will be wonderful autumn days, the trees ablaze with oranges and reds, and just enough of a chill in the air to make us throw on a sweater? Will there be bright, hot, sunny days, when the summer air smells of the country, and a cool breeze stirs the leaves on the trees? A spring, with thousands of spring colors and flowers? Lovely white winter snowstorms?

The answer to all these questions is yes! You bet there will. God never discards his creations, but only changes them to make them better. There is no reason to believe that he won't keep all the things in this life that are gorgeous already.

And that includes canyons and glaciers and valleys and oceans and beaches and mountains and rivers, and everything else that is beautiful on Earth. You see, human beings already believe that when they "commune with nature," they are somehow closer to their creator. Some people take the concept too far and assert that nature itself is God. While we certainly don't agree with the pantheists, we recognize that there is a fundamental truth that they are touching, namely, that one of the ways we can come closest to experiencing the majesty of God is through his creation. Psalm 19 says, "The heavens are telling the glory of God; and the firmament proclaims his handiwork." That's exactly what I mean.

And that's why these things that we love so much on Earth will continue to exist in heaven. They themselves are signs of God. It's similar to what we said before about human beings. When you enter heaven, you will enter with your true identity, as the best man or woman you can possibly be. The "new earth" will be at its best too. It will retain all the amazing and wonderful aspects of its present state, but will no longer manifest all its unpleasant, wayward characteristics. How, exactly? There won't be any earthquakes in heaven or any other violent "natural" catastrophes, no killing winters, no devastating hurricanes. It will be completely subject to God's benevolent will.[4]

Now it goes without saying that this transformation will not just be limited to keeping the good and eliminating the bad. God is much too imaginative for that. We've said that in heaven we'll be able to experience a whole new variety of sights, sounds, smells, and textures. Along with that we are going to see a whole new variety of created *things*.

If there's one conclusion you should be able to draw from this discussion, it's that God is an artist. A great artist. I don't have to describe all the thousands of species of animals, insects, plants, and flowers that exist in the world to illustrate God's creativity. Just take a walk through any botanical garden or any good zoo and you can see that God has an absolutely insatiable love for inventing the most amazing things. Sometimes, when we observe a particularly interesting-looking creature, like an aardvark or sea walrus, you can almost hear God chuckling during the act of creation. God has a sense of humor and a flair for living that we don't often credit him for. It's time we started.

My point in all this is that God is going to continue creating things forever. In the next couple of chapters, we're going to be talking a great deal about the kinds of living beings that will populate heaven. For now, though, it's enough to understand that heaven will be full of all sorts of animals, vegetables, and minerals, the likes of which have never been seen.

Finally, we've spoken a lot about nature and the natural elements, but it would be a great mistake to think of heaven as one colossal nature preserve. For some that might indeed be paradise, but for others, it's not very fulfilling. In fact, it might actually seem a bit boring. Nature will indeed make up one part of heaven, but there's something else equally exciting.

In the Book of Revelation, which tells us what the future holds for the world, part of heaven is called the "New Jerusalem." The description provided by the Apostle John, who wrote the book at the end of the first century, is one of the most aesthetically sumptuous in the Bible:

> And I saw the holy city . . . Its light was like a
> precious stone's . . . and it had a wall great and
> high with twelve gates, and at the gates, twelve
> angels . . . the material of its wall was jasper;
> but the city itself was pure gold . . . the founda-
> tions of the wall of the city were adorned with
> every kind of precious stone. The first . . .

jasper, the second, sapphire, the third, agate, the fourth, emerald . . . And the twelve gates were twelve pearls . . . And the street of the city was pure gold, like transparent glass.[5]

Even accounting for the symbolic language and poetry of the passage, it should be obvious that when John is describing our dwelling place in heaven, he is talking about a real, honest-to-goodness city.

And doesn't that make sense? After all, if we're going to have our bodies in heaven, we'll all need a place to live. Even if we have the ability to move through solid objects, there are still times when we're going to want to be inside instead of outside. That's our nature as human beings.

So heaven must contain a city of sorts. An amazingly vast city. And inside that city, there will be buildings and houses; and human beings are going to live in those houses. I know people don't usually think of heaven being made up of city blocks with homes, but that's what it's going to be like.

Aside from what Revelation teaches about the New Jerusalem being great, brilliant, and beautiful, no one can say for sure what kind of city it will be. But we do have several clues on which to base some exciting speculations.

We know, for instance, that God never wastes anything. We know that when he creates, he does it for eternity. We also know that God gave mankind the power to create as well. That's one of the things we mean when we say we are made in the "image and likeness" of God. When humans act creatively, when we build things, make things, invent things, and imagine things, we are truly acting like God and using his power within us to the fullest.

What this means is that the things we make in this life have value beyond the day to day. Inasmuch as we are acting like God when we create, we also have the Godlike power to create things that are everlasting. What that comes down to in practical terms is that in building up our own cities, God may actually be allowing us, in some mysterious way, to build up heaven.

Think about what an amazing concept that is. The work we are doing in this life may be helping to create the kingdom of heaven.

The implications for us are staggering. It means that heaven may very well be made up of cities that we are very familiar with, because we live in them *now!* Like the rest of creation, they too might be transformed, although they will still be our cities. And I don't mean just the cities we've built up in the last few years, I mean all the cities that have been built up in all times by all peoples. There's no reason why God would let any of the magnificent cultures and civilizations that we have created go to waste.

That's not his style. They may be dust now, but God is only holding them, waiting to give them back to us, brand spanking new, in heaven. It's so important to grasp this concept: *Nothing is ever lost with God.*

Imagine all the incredible possibilities. We'll be able to see ancient Rome again, not in ruins, but clad in all its golden splendor. We'll be able to see the Pyramids and the Sphinx just as they were on the day they were built. We'll be able to view the Parthenon with all its marble columns and statues intact. We'll be able to walk through the streets of old Paris, or Renaissance Florence, or the China of the Ming Dynasty.

Likewise, ancient Greeks and Romans who rise from the dead on the Last Day will get to see the skyline of Manhattan. And yes, why shouldn't it be true that in God's heaven, the World Trade Center will rise up again? I know this all seems incredible, but heaven *is* incredible.

And we've only just scratched the surface. You know, one of the saddest sights is an amusement park in the winter, devoid of people and totally silent. The picture of heaven we've painted in this chapter is vast in scope and contains an endless variety of things for humans to do and enjoy. But as of yet, it's still empty of occupants. Let's talk a little about the people who are going to reside there—our traveling companions.

CHAPTER 4

Our Fellow Travelers

A few years ago I was in Rome to attend some meetings. It was a business trip, so I was traveling alone. Soon after arriving, I got word that one of my meetings had been canceled, and I suddenly had an entire afternoon to myself. I decided to take the opportunity to see some of the sights. I was excited by the thought of spending the time alone—doing what I wanted to do, taking things at my own pace. It was an adventure, and I felt like some character out of a Hemingway novel, going off by myself and having a great time.

Somewhere halfway through the day, though, I noticed something surprising. I noticed that I wasn't really enjoying myself all that much. Every time I saw something interesting, the thought would pop into my mind, "My dad would love this," or "It's too bad my brothers aren't here to see that." When I stopped at a lovely outdoor café in front of the Trevi fountain, I thought it would be great to have a delicious spaghetti lunch with some red wine. But as I sat there on that beautiful sunny day, looking at that incredible fountain, listening to all the happy people around me, I kept coming back to one thought: "I wish my wife were here."

Has this ever happened to you? Have you ever been off alone and said to yourself, "I have to come back here with so-and-so," or "I can't believe my friend isn't here right now to enjoy this"? Have you ever been to a nice place and realized that you really weren't having much fun, that the experience was somehow incomplete, because you were there alone? If so, then you understand a basic human need: the need to share good times with the people you love.

Now I'm not saying it isn't possible to enjoy yourself when you're alone. Of course it is. Human beings have a need for solitude, too—at least occasionally. Sometimes being alone is necessary in order to preserve our sanity; sometimes we just have to take the time to collect our thoughts in silence and nurture ourselves.

But first in the hierarchy of human needs is still the necessity for companionship and connectedness. In its highest expression, we call this love. Human beings absolutely require this in order to be happy. That's the way we're built. Another way of saying it is that we are, by nature, social creatures.

How can we know this for sure? Well, the first evidence was given to us right at the start of human history. Whether or not you believe in a literal interpretation of the Book of Genesis, the fact is that one of the main points of the story is that God created the first woman — Eve — because the first man was lonely. God just couldn't stand the thought of Adam being by himself.[1]

But it goes even deeper than that. We've said previously that human beings are made in the image and likeness of God.[2] Did you know that God himself is a "social" being?

If you're a Christian, you've read in the Bible and heard at church that God is "Father, Son, and Holy Spirit." Christ referred to this relationship many times during the course of his earthly ministry. We call this the mystery of the Holy Trinity. While the various Christian denominations may have their disagreements on a slew of other issues, they all agree on this one central doctrine of faith: God is one, but at the same time, he is three.[3]

This is an important point to grasp. Christians believe there is only one true God. And this one God is made of one substance, if you will. In every sense of the word, he is one being. But he is also, in some way that we can't fully comprehend, three distinct persons within that one being.

If you don't understand that, don't worry, you're in good company. For two thousand years, theologians have pondered that biblical truth. And there are hundreds of excellent books that attempt to give us a better understanding of the relationship between the "persons" who make up the one "godhead."

Obviously, it's beyond the scope of this book to delve into that grand mystery. The point we need to comprehend, though, is that God himself is a plurality within a unity. God himself—in his very nature—is a *family*. He has within him various relationships. He is not solitary.

How does all this relate to heaven?

Well, if God is a social being, and we are made in God's image, then we too, by extension, must be social beings. We are not meant to live a solitary existence, either here or in the next world. Therefore, when we finally arrive at the happiest place in all of creation, does it make sense that we're going to spend our time there alone?

A tremendous part of the happiness and pleasure that we are destined to experience in heaven will not come from our incredible new bodies, or from our incredible new surroundings. Rather, it will come from the *people* we are with, from our fellow travelers.

Now most travel guides don't usually discuss the

people who accompany us on vacation. That's because there's no way of knowing who, exactly, is going to be traveling with us on any particular trip. But that's where this guidebook differs. For the trip we make to the after-life is not unique to any specific person or family. On the contrary, all of us—and that means billions of people throughout the long span of history—are headed off on the "ultimate vacation" together.

As the saying goes, we're all in the same boat. No matter who you are, no matter whether you believe in God or not, no matter if you are good or evil—you are go-ing to experience the resurrection and Final Judgment. Hopefully, when you arrive at your final destination point you'll be checking into a hotel in heaven! But whatever the case, you're going *somewhere* with your newly minted body—and it won't be some black void of nothingness, as atheists believe.

Christianity has always taught that at an appointed day in history, known only to God, the world will come to an end and there will be a Last Judgment, during which time the souls of all the departed will be judged according to their life on Earth. At this judgment, they will be re-united with their bodies, and will spend eternity either in heaven, with God, or in that unpleasant place below called hell, which none of us likes talking much about.

When we think about this whole subject, a lot of

dark, frightening images can come into our mind. Some friends have told me they've even had nightmares about the resurrection, and that they picture graves opening up, and people in tattered, decayed suits climbing out from the dirt. If you're not careful, it's possible to conceive of the resurrection as a scene from a low-budget horror movie.

Well, do you think that's the kind of gruesome start God has in mind for opening day in paradise? Do you think that the first thing God's going to do after he gives us back our bodies is scare us half to death?

I'll tell you exactly what the resurrection is going to be like. In the Gospel of Mark, there is a wonderful scene where Christ raises a twelve-year-old girl from the dead.[4] It starts in the house of the girl who has died, with all sorts of wailing and crying going on in the background. The girl's mother and father are understandably distraught, and the family is completely broken. Amidst the confusion, Christ very calmly tells the parents not to be upset, because the girl is "not dead, but only sleeping."

You can imagine the anger this remark causes in the people gathered around. They start to yell at him. After all, where does this crazy stranger get off saying the child isn't dead? How dare he raise their hopes that way? What is he trying to do to them? Christ's response is simply to order everyone to leave except the mother and father and his own disciples. He quietly sits next to the girl, who is lying there dead, and gently takes her hand. Then he very softly says to her, *Arise, little girl.*

Immediately the girl opens her eyes and begins to move.

That's the way our own resurrection is going to be. It won't be gory, with scary music in the background and graves opening up. When we rise from the dead, the experience is going to be soft, gentle, and instantaneous, just like the scene in the Bible. At the end of the world, Christ is simply going to whisper one solitary word, *arise,* and in a twinkling of an eye we will all come back to life with our bodies fully intact and brand new.[5] And when we open our eyes at that moment and look around, there won't be a tombstone in sight. Why? Because there are no cemeteries in heaven.

Is all this hard for you to believe? Some people have trouble accepting the fact that once they are dead and buried they can ever be brought back to life. They wonder how God is going to "put the pieces back together," especially after their body has undergone decomposition, or if there's been a cremation. Well, let me ask you a simple question. Where were you exactly one hundred years ago? For most people, the answer is: nowhere. You didn't have a body; you didn't have a soul. You didn't exist at all.

Well, if God could pull you out of nonexistence, and

create the person you are, with all your characteristics, all your emotions, and all your experiences, why would it be so difficult for him to bring you back to life once you already exist? Next to the awesome act of creation, resurrection is a snap.

It's important to understand that this belief we have in the resurrection is at the central core of Christianity. It's what all the worship, all the prayers, all the supplications, all the acts of devotion, all the practices of religion are all about. It's the good news that's proclaimed in the Gospels. It's the meaning of Easter. It's the reason martyrs through the centuries have been able to joyfully accept suffering and even torturous deaths. It's the reason Christians today can handle being mocked, ridiculed, and harassed by a society that disdains them for their values.

It would be easy enough not to believe in the resurrection. After all, many people in the world don't. Some religions, for example, teach that life is cyclical, and that we get many chances to go around the wheel of existence. They believe that when we die, we must come back to life again in another form, like a fish or an insect, and that we must keep coming back until we get it right. Other religions teach that once we die we become part of nature—part of some great, unseen force of energy. Others still are very unclear as to what they believe about the afterlife.

Not Christianity. If there's one thing we're sure

about, it's death and resurrection. We believe with complete certitude that: 1) we are created out of nothing; 2) we live only once and die only once; 3) after we complete our life on Earth we are judged by God; and finally, 4) we experience bodily resurrection *and live forever*—either in heaven or in hell.[6]

That's the whole story of our existence. That's what it all comes down to. In his first letter to the Corinthians, St. Paul sums up this rock-solid, uncompromising belief in the resurrection:

> How can some of you say there is no resurrection of the dead? If there is no resurrection of the dead, then Christ has not been raised; and if Christ has not been raised, then our preaching is in vain and your faith is in vain, your faith is futile and you are still in your sins . . . For if this is the only life we have hoped for in Christ, we are all men most to be pitied . . . If the dead are not raised, "Let us eat and drink, for tomorrow we die."[7]

That's how black-and-white we are about the resurrection. Without it, there is simply no Christian religion.

Now what does all this mean in practical terms for our life in heaven? Simply this: we are once again going to see all the people we knew and loved who have died. If you're reading this now and your mother has died, rest assured that you're going to see her again. If your father has died, you're going to see him again. If your brothers or sisters have died, you're going to see them again. As long as these loved ones make it into heaven, we're going to see them *all* again.

This belief of ours has been stated so often and so flippantly that it's almost lost its emotional power. We've got to stop and think about it. It's vital that you visualize in your mind what the *scene* in heaven is going to look like the first day you arrive. It's important to see all the details, to take in all the sights, sounds, and sensations. You have to make it real, because it's going to *be* real. The problem for us weak-minded humans is that it's very easy for us to fall into the habit of picturing heaven in the same old gray, lifeless way. It's easy for us to dismiss our deepest yearnings as mere "wishful thinking." We can't allow that to happen, because it's not true.

Christianity hasn't managed to survive two millennia on wishful thinking. The early Christian families that were fed to the lions didn't go singing to their horrible deaths because of wishful thinking. The great saints down through the ages who willingly endured agonizing martyrdoms didn't do so because of wishful thinking. They were all able to live and die courageously because they knew the resurrection was a *fact*. We can't let ourselves forget what they knew so well.

Let's step into the future for a moment. Think about what we've discussed in the last few chapters, and now, try to make it real. Close your eyes and do your best to make the experience of heaven *personal*.

You know that when you see your friends and relatives there someday, you're going to see these people *in the flesh*. You'll be able to recognize them and they're going to recognize you. Imagine what that first moment will be like — the first instant when you see your mom, your dad, your husband, or your grandmother. It may be that you haven't seen them in years and years, and now they're right there, standing two feet in front of you. What do you think your reaction will be?

Remember, you're going to have your body in heaven, so you won't be restricted to merely contemplating or praying for them. You'll be able to get physical. You'll be able to run up to them the second you see them and jump into their waiting arms and embrace them and kiss them.

You'll be able to cry with joy when you're hugging them. You'll be able to feel the warmth of their bodies again. You'll be able to hear their *voices* — voices you haven't heard in so long.

You'll be able to have a conversation with them, and

tell them all that's happened in your life since you last saw them. You'll be able to hear them laugh again and watch them smile again, hold their hands and squeeze them tight, and put your head on their shoulders.

Best of all, you'll be able to *be* with them again. *That's* what the resurrection means. The Bible describes heaven as a banquet.[8] Well, that's the same as saying God is going to throw a big party for us! It means there will be plenty of people, plenty of family, plenty of laughter, plenty of conversation, plenty of music, plenty of togetherness, plenty of noise.

There's going to be electricity in the air that first day in heaven. People who haven't seen each other for years are going to be reunited. And they're going to be young again! People who were born blind will open their eyes for the first time and see the faces of their loved ones. People who were crippled and deformed will run through the streets. People who suffered with debilitating diseases all their lives on Earth are going to be more vibrant, robust, and healthy than the greatest Olympic athlete.

Imagine the emotional intensity of that experience. Imagine the river of tears that is going to flow. Imagine how loud it's going to be, with all those billions of people laughing, crying, talking, and carrying on. It's truly going to be a sight to behold.

Some people can't imagine our all-powerful God

throwing a fun-filled bash like we've described. How ridiculous! God is also *all-loving,* and knowing how much he enjoys seeing us happy, do you really think he's going to let us miss out on a moment like that? Not a chance.

And the best thing of all is that once we experience those first precious hours, that first wild reunion, we will have completed only our first morning in heaven.

CHAPTER 5

Till Death Do Us Part?

One of the nicest things that can happen to us when we're on a trip is to meet other vacationers and become friends with them. It's much easier to do this on a cruise, when we're seated with the same people night after night. But it can happen anywhere, especially if we tend to be the more sociable type. Sometimes—though not often—we can even form relationships that last beyond a particular trip. I know two couples who have been vacationing together for more than twenty years, all because they struck up a friendship one summer day while watching their children splash about in a motel pool.

It's marvelous when these kinds of long-lasting relationships form. And it's only natural for us to wonder, what kinds of relationships are we going to experience on our eternal vacation?

As we saw in the last chapter, the teaching on the resurrection of the body is one of the most consoling doctrines of the Christian faith. It's great news for all of us who are either afraid of death or who desperately miss friends and relatives who have gone on before us. But it can make us nervous as well, especially in regard to this whole idea of postresurrection relationships. After all, our bodies will be undergoing some pretty incredible changes. Is there any chance that these alterations are going to affect the close ties we've forged here on Earth?

I think much of the apprehension we feel about this topic comes from an overinterpretation of something Christ said in the Bible. The gospels of Matthew, Mark, and Luke relate an interesting incident concerning the Sadducees, a Jewish sect that did not believe in the resurrection.[1] At one point, members of the sect attempt to trip up Jesus by quizzing him about the afterlife. They tell him a story about a woman who had been married seven times to seven different men, each of whom had died. Which husband, they ask, will she be married to in heaven? Jesus responds by saying that *no one* is going to be married in heaven, that marriage itself is only meant to last during our lifetime in this world.

Now, it's possible to come away from this story a little upset. After all, what if we like being married? What if we've spent thirty or forty or fifty years with our spouse and have shared millions of wonderful memories with them—memories of being young and buying a house together; of having children; of enjoying holidays and vacations together; of seeing the kids grow up and get married; of being just two people alone again, taking care of each other? Is all that lost forever once we die?

And while we're at it, if there isn't going to be any marriage in the afterlife, what other kinds of relationships does God intend to erase? Does this mean there will be no fathers and mothers in heaven—or grandparents, cousins, siblings, uncles, and aunts? If you believe that the relationships most important to you in life are going to end the moment you die, that alone indicates that your picture of heaven is pretty dismal.

That's a shame, because our relationships in heaven are going to be fabulous! All Jesus said was that there isn't going to be any marriage in heaven. Before we jump to all kinds of conclusions, let's take a look at the institution of marriage and see if we can understand why Jesus said it won't exist in the afterlife.

We know that people get married for many reasons—love, passion, romance, companionship, etcetera—and all of these are good and worthy motivations. But we often forget that one of the main purposes of marriage—

indeed one of the reasons God created it in the first place—is to help us get to heaven.

By joining two people together as one, God gives us a built-in lifetime assistant who can help us overcome all the obstacles, challenges, and suffering that we are bound to face in this world.[2] The assistance itself comes about through the practice of true love.

Now, the word *love* today is very misunderstood. It has been watered down and trivialized so much that it means practically nothing. Love is *not* mushy feelings. Nor is it two amorous teenagers looking into each other's eyes on a moonlit night at the beach and then ripping each other's clothes off. No matter how intense their declarations of love might be, this activity falls under the category of passion.

True love has only one definition: selfless, self-sacrificing giving. It's getting up at four in the morning when the baby is crying and feeding him so that your wife can sleep; it's letting your husband put on the football game Monday night instead of insisting you both watch your favorite sitcom; it's taking your wife out for dinner and dancing on the weekend when you really just want to sit in front of the TV and spin the remote control. It's doing all the things you don't want to do for the sake of the other person. It's putting that person's wants, needs, and desires ahead of yours.[3]

When you love your spouse with a spirit of selfless giving, you are imitating Christ, because that is exactly the kind of love he showed for us. "This is my body," he said the night before he was crucified, "given up for you."[4] I'm sure it wasn't a pleasant experience being nailed to a cross. But he endured the suffering, so that we could one day experience the joy of resurrection and heaven. By sacrificing himself, he was putting *our* interests ahead of his.

Marriage provides us with an abundance of opportunities to exercise the same kind of Christlike love. (All of us who are married can attest to this fact!) If we follow through on our wedding vows, we have no choice but to become more holy. And when we're holy, we're on the fast track to heaven.

Having children is the other major reason God invented marriage.[5] A husband and wife make love and with the help of God create another human being. God provides the new baby's soul; the parents provide the new baby's body (this too with God's help, of course). By joining in the act of creation, the couple becomes more like God. Moreover they assist him to fill the Earth with people, and thus to populate heaven. And children themselves provide us with the greatest opportunity to practice self-sacrificing love. We don't need to go into the thousands of different ways moms and dads put the lives of their kids before their own. It's the essence of the entire relationship.

All these things help foster greater holiness, and thus cut a direct path for us to heaven. In the final analysis, this is the only true standard by which we can judge whether or not a marriage has been successful. The definition of a great marriage is one that leads both husband and wife to heaven.

Once that objective is achieved, however, and we finally arrive safely in paradise, there isn't a need for "marriage" anymore. Marriage will have served its purpose. And this is where some of us get worried.

It's difficult to spend your life with someone and then face the prospect of having to part with him or her at death. Despite what Jesus said, we can't help but ask, isn't there a way for God to salvage the relationship?

And indeed, there is! In fact, there's never really been any cause for concern, because while the structure, institution, and sacrament of marriage will no longer be required in heaven, the *relationship* between the two people will continue forever. We can compare it to a game of tennis between two friends. When they are playing on the tennis court, we call them tennis partners. They dress a certain way, use certain equipment, abide by certain rules, stay within certain boundary lines. Once the game is over, however, they leave the court and cease to be tennis partners. But that doesn't mean their relationship ceases. It doesn't mean, for instance, that they necessarily get into their cars and drive their separate ways. It doesn't mean that they stop knowing each other or loving each other.

Indeed, the two people may even have a much deeper relationship *off* the tennis court. That's the way it is with married couples in heaven.

Are we going to know our husbands and wives in heaven? Of course. And yes, we're going to have special relationships with them. Will they be the same kinds of relationships they were on Earth? No. But they will be special and unique. How could it be otherwise? We shared all those wonderful memories with them; and besides, they personally helped us to get to heaven. Don't you think that counts for anything with God?

Part of the confusion we have about this comes from a misunderstanding of the way we're going to love others in the afterlife. We've heard it said so often that God is love and that heaven is going to be full of love, that we think human emotions are going to be the same across the board. We picture heaven as being filled with robotlike creatures that go around "loving" everything and everyone in the same way. But the truth is, there will be different levels of affection in the afterlife. Love in heaven will be universal, not communistic.

Christ himself tried to demonstrate this to us. Remember in the Gospel of St. John how many times the evangelist refers to himself as the "disciple whom Jesus loved"?[6] What did he mean by that? I used to think that John was being a little bit arrogant and presumptuous. After all, didn't Jesus love everyone?

It wasn't till later that I realized John wasn't bragging at all. He was being justifiably proud of something that was true. Of course Jesus loved all the apostles. But he had greater emotional affection for John. There's nothing wrong with that. Human beings do it all the time. Painters and musicians always have special affection for a particular work they've created. Charles Dickens, for example, loved all the characters in his novels and stories, but his favorite was always David Copperfield.

Well, God is allowed to have favorites among his creations too.

But to "have" favorites doesn't mean that you "play" favorites. To love someone with greater emotional intensity does not mean that you don't love everyone. Parents understand this better than anyone. You may be particularly "close" to one of your children, but that doesn't mean you wouldn't give your life for all of them.

Personalitywise, Jesus seems to have *liked* John more than the other apostles. On the night prior to his crucifixion, John was the one who was privileged to lay his head on the Lord's breast, comforting him before his agony in the Garden. Obviously, the two shared an intimate bond as friends. But this didn't stop Christ from naming Peter—after his remarkable profession of faith—the "rock" on which he would build his church.[7] Peter probably had certain leadership qualities that John lacked. Jesus took that into account, notwithstanding his affection for John. And while Christ, being truly human, formed certain bonds with and attachments to specific people, that didn't stop him, as our divine parent, from sacrificing his life for *all* people.

My point here is that while there will certainly be a new "brotherhood of man" in heaven, that doesn't preclude the existence of special relationships between individuals. It's imperative that we understand this. Happy memories are not lost in heaven; family ties are not broken; intimacy is not decreased. On the contrary, friendships formed on Earth will continue forever, because bonds of love and affection are eternal. None of the feelings of attachment we have now will be watered down in heaven.

Remember, nothing good is ever lost with God. Not material goods, not spiritual goods, not relational goods.

Will the relationships we presently have change in heaven? Of course they will, at least to some extent, because the dynamics of heavenly life are different from the dynamics of our earthly existence. For one thing, they'll be much deeper than they are now. How so?

On Earth, the good and bad in people are so mixed

up together. We get moody, depressed, and nasty at the drop of a hat, and it's hard for other people to know how to deal with us. Also, there are so many external forces pressing against us on a daily basis—bills, car troubles, problems at work, problems with our kids—that we can't help having arguments with each other. In heaven, we'll be at our best all the time, and our only problem will be figuring out what exciting thing to do next. This will eliminate the bulk of the strain we experience in our relationships now.

On Earth, we rarely understand all the psychological reasons for negative behavior. When people we're close to do bad things to us, we get angry and form animosities. Even in our most wonderful relationships, we have scar tissue from past wrongs that have been inflicted on us. In heaven, God reveals all our inner motivations. We'll know why people we love acted in certain ways that were hurtful to us. We'll see clearly that it was because they were insecure, or because they were wounded themselves, or because of something that happened to them in their childhood. So many of the things that are not communicated now will be understood then. And for the first time we'll also see *our own* weakness clearly. When we realize just how much God has forgiven us, the sins that others have committed against us will seem trivial.

You see, no matter how much we love a particular

person on Earth, it's still like looking at someone through a dirty window. Our psychologies, our environment, our past experiences, and our weaknesses all get in the way to create a cloudy barrier between us. We see enough of the other person to love them, but it's still a distorted view. No matter how well we *think* we know them, we can't see clearly and neither can they.

When we get to heaven, however, it's as if the window were not only cleaned, but removed altogether. Any lingering animosities we carried in our hearts will be obliterated forever. That's why the relationships we have in the afterlife will be deeper and better than ever before.

In this regard, people often wonder if there's going to be sex in heaven. After all, if heaven is as physical as we've made it out to be, doesn't it make sense that we'll be able to love each other in a physical way?

No one is really sure of the answer to that question. On the one hand, we know that human sexuality—when it takes place within the bonds of a legitimate marriage—is beautiful and pleasurable, and that it allows us to share in God's power of creation. Every single denomination of Christianity believes that sex is holy, not evil—that it is a gift from God. (We know it comes from God for the simple reason that human beings haven't invented anything near as good!)

We also know that nothing good is ever lost with God, so it would seem that the pleasure humans derive from sexuality will somehow be retained in the afterlife. However, since there won't be any marriage in heaven, nor the need for children, we have a dilemma. God certainly wouldn't want to trivialize the gift of sex by allowing it to be used by random partners, indiscriminately. He doesn't like it when we do that here, and he certainly won't allow it in heaven.

There are only two possible answers. Either God will find a way for us to retain the pleasurable sensations and unitive qualities inherent in the act of lovemaking without the sinfulness that accompanies sex outside marriage on Earth—or he will substitute something better in its place.

Now what can be better than sex, in terms of physical pleasure?

I don't know, but then again, I'm not God. People who dismiss the idea of sex in heaven usually cite examples like that of the little boy who only wants to play with his video games. When you tell him that one day he's going to lose all interest in such childish pursuits and instead prefer things like books, work, and girls, he grimaces in disbelief. *Girls? Yuck!*

And yet we know very well what happens when that

little boy reaches puberty. It may be the same with us in heaven. God may have something planned for us that is as far above sex as girls are above Nintendo.

We'll all know, soon enough. We'll know the answer to this question about sex in heaven, and we'll know exactly how our relationships there will differ from those on Earth. But whatever we learn, the main point is that the relationships themselves will remain intact.

Ten billion years from today, your mom will still be your mom—and she'll be able to talk to you in ways that only a mother can talk to her child. Ten billion years from today, your brothers will still be your brothers, and you'll have a certain camaraderie with them that only siblings can enjoy. Ten billion years from today, you'll be able to gather around a table together for a Thanksgiving meal with your family, the same way you do now and have done so many times in the past.

The real difference will be that when you have that Thanksgiving dinner in heaven, everyone you remember from your childhood will be there. The people who used to gather around that table but have left you one by one over the years will be sitting there alive again, and smiling back at you.

In light of that incredible truth, other differences don't mean all that much, anyway.

CHAPTER 6

Do All Dogs Go to Heaven?

Since we've been describing heaven as an all-inclusive vacation, it's only fair to ask: Are pets allowed at this resort?

After all, it would be hard to overestimate the importance of animals—particularly our own pets—in our lives. They keep us company when our family and friends have left us; they're loyal when everyone else has deserted us. They're our companions, our protectors, our buddies, and our confidants. No one—not even our spouses—is ever happier to see us after we return home from a hard day's work. Right or wrong, it's sometimes true that we're closer to our dogs and cats than we are to other people.

Of course we *want* animals to be with us in heaven.

We can't imagine being perfectly happy in heaven without them.

And yet, throughout the history of theology, there's been a question about the ultimate fate of these wonderful creatures. A few spiritual writers have actually said that they didn't believe animals could go to heaven. And while no denomination of Christianity has ever conclusively accepted their assertions, there's always been a bit of a debate surrounding the subject. The argument made by the skeptical theologians is that animals are not made in the image and likeness of God, and therefore do not have immortal souls. According to this way of thinking, only human beings are meant for eternity. After all, that's why Christ died for us. If animals were able to live forever, our intrinsic value would somehow be decreased. The special place reserved for us from the beginning of time would be threatened.

But do you know something? The theologians who posit this argument are like brilliant mathematicians who formulate brilliant equations, and then get the simplest answers wrong. They're correct about the calculus of religion, but they falter when it comes to easy addition.

Will our pets be allowed to go to heaven? Of course! The question theologians should be asking is: Why not?

After all, God can do whatever he wants. That's the most fundamental point in all theology. The Almighty

Creator of the universe, maker of the sun, the moon, and the stars, is not bound by any limitations; he's not restricted to acting within the confines of a syllogism, or any other logical construct created by human beings. Arguing that the soul animals possess is not made of "immortal" substance is secondary to the discussion. What counts is God's absolute power and his overriding desire to make us happy.

Thus, if God wants to be generous to all his creatures, that's his prerogative. If he wants to allow animals to live in heaven, then animals will be in heaven. Period.

The idea that our existence is somehow trivialized if animals are permitted to live forever is absurd. The Bible makes it clear that there is going to be lush vegetation in heaven. Well, Christ obviously didn't die on the cross to redeem vegetation. But that won't stop him from making heaven green with foliage so that human beings can be happier there.

Do you think God is going to let some shrub experience life everlasting and refuse the same gift to a puppy? Is that consistent with the way God acts? Just because we are created in God's image and animals are not doesn't mean that God can't give animals special permission to share eternity with us, just as he is going to give special permission to the trees and leaves and grass and flowers. They don't have immortal souls, either, but they are still part of God's creation. And as we've said many times now, God doesn't throw away the good things he creates.

Now don't get the idea here that I am making some silly argument that anything that seems good to me, in the subjective sense, will have eternal life. I can imagine some people asserting that since the great pleasure of their life was marijuana, and since God created marijuana plants, they can look forward to getting perpetually stoned in the afterlife ("heaven's gonna be a blast!"). There are plenty of pleasurable activities we can indulge in now that are not "good," but are, in fact, quite sinful. It goes without saying that they will have no place in the life to come. In heaven, there will be a total eradication of all sin and sinfulness.

Animals, however, are not sinful. In fact, all the evidence points to the fact that they are especially dear to God's heart. (Psalm 36 says plainly: "You care for people and animals alike, O Lord.")[1] Just look at how he's used them so many times in the history of the world to reveal his divine plan. Did you know that there are over a hundred and twenty species of animals named in the Bible? All you have to do is flip through the Good Book, and you'll read about birds and camels and foxes and horses and leopards and lions and sparrows. They're all over the place.

Recall the first Nativity scene. Besides Jesus's parents, the only living creatures to be present at this most solemn moment in human history were the animals in the stable. Bear in mind this was the single greatest thing ever to happen to mankind; God actually became one of us. And yet, the only living beings allowed to witness the event were cows and sheep.

Now go back even farther. Go back to the one time in history when God condemned our planet, the one time he destroyed life on Earth and killed all but a few human beings. Remember the story of Noah? Well, who were the only creatures—besides Noah and his family—that God deemed worthy of saving? Who were the only creatures that had tickets to the ark? It was the animals! Was there ever a more telling sign that God thinks highly of our four-legged friends?

And animals are not just "mentioned" in the Bible. They play key roles in all of revelation.[2] If it weren't for a "great fish," there'd be no book of Jonah. If it weren't for a donkey, Mary wouldn't have gotten to Bethlehem. If it weren't for a flock of sheep, the shepherds wouldn't have received the first Christmas Eve message from the angels. If it weren't for a colt, Christ wouldn't have been able to ride into Jerusalem on Palm Sunday.

God loves to use animals to help him achieve his plan, and he loves to use them as symbols of that plan.[3] The lamb, for example, is a profoundly important symbol of the deliverance of God's people from bondage; it also symbolizes Christ's paschal sacrifice. And we all know that the dove is the symbol of peace—as well as a sign of the presence of the Holy Spirit.

The question is, if animals have played such a critical role in God's revelation up till now, why wouldn't they continue to play some kind of role in heaven? Part of the reason for their existence is to give us pleasure and joy. That's what they do now, and that's what they're going to do in the future. It's that simple. Think about the heaven that we've described in this book. Think about how colorful and fun-filled it's going to be. Does it make sense that animals would be left out of that picture?

Even if we put revelation to the side for a moment, we can still come to this same conclusion. Most of us have had a pet at one time or another. When those pets die, it hurts. But we saw in the last chapter that there is a false finality about death. When people we love die, they leave a terrible void in our lives, and we feel that their death is so absolutely final and irrevocable that we can barely breathe. Yet, though our emotions tell us one thing, we also know that there's more to the story. Our faith assures us that in reality—the deepest, truest reality—all those people we lost are going to come back into our lives again. Animals are certainly not on the same level as human beings; but we still know deep down that God has something more planned for them than the mere twelve or thirteen years they have with us on Earth.

We spoke a little about that first morning in heaven—the first moments of that remarkable reunion, when sons and daughters reunite with their mothers and fathers after ages of being apart. Well, we left out one important detail in that description. We didn't say that in the midst of all the excitement, in the midst of all the laughing and crying, just as you're hugging your mom or dad for the first time, you shouldn't be surprised if you suddenly feel something wet licking your hand. You shouldn't be shocked if you feel a paw anxiously poking at your leg. When you look down, you can well guess what you're going to see—your old, faithful dog. Only he won't be old and sick, like the last time you saw him. He'll be young again, and he'll be as vibrant and alive and exuberant as he was years ago, when you used to run with him and play with him for hours.

This is not pie-in-the-sky, wishful thinking. This is the truth. This is Christianity. Heaven is going to be filled with animals. Every single pet you ever had in your life is going to be there. Every dog, every cat, every parakeet, every bunny, every goldfish, every gerbil. *God loses nothing.*

And the pattern we've seen God use for the Earth and for human beings is the pattern he's going to use for the animals, too. In heaven, they will be essentially the same creatures as they are now, only they will be made *new*. How so?

Nowhere else on Earth is God's artistry more apparent than in the animal kingdom. Just take a walk through a zoo or an aquarium and see what I mean: giraffes, zebras, lions, tigers, polar bears, leopards, butterflies, blue jays, cardinals, peacocks, flamingos, swordfish, dolphins, killer whales; the list goes on and on. Michelangelo on his best day couldn't duplicate the magnificence of line, color, and form manifest in God's animal creations.

God's not about to deprive heaven of all that color and beauty. Chances are he's going to keep those marvelous creatures pretty much the way they look now. After all, they've already attained a level of perfection in their outward appearance, why would they have to be changed?

What will be altered is their behavior. All the "rules" animals live by on Earth will no longer apply in heaven. There won't be any "food chain," for instance. Nor will there be a need to "eat or be eaten." "Survival of the fittest" will not have any role to play in the afterlife. In heaven there won't be any need to eat at all. Therefore animals won't have to hunt each other. They won't be dangerous. The Old Testament says that "on that day, the wolf and the lamb will lie down together, and the leopard and goat will be at peace."[4]

Walking down a street in heaven is going to be like going through one of those natural wild habitats, only there won't be a need for any separation between the animals and us. We'll be able to play with the bear and lion cubs as easily as we play with our puppies and kittens today.

But of course there's more to heaven than just this. We should know by now that God's always got something surprising for us up his sleeve.

Scientists tell us the Earth was created some 4.6 billion years ago. Human beings came on the scene a mere million years ago. If you accept this as true (and I realize some creationists dispute it), then you have to ask why God worked the chronology that way. What was he doing all that time before human history began? What was so important that it required 4.6 billion years of effort on his part?

I'll tell you a little secret. *He was working on heaven.*

During that time volcanoes erupted, glaciers moved, and continental plates shifted. Millions of summers and winters went by, and the Earth went through massive geological and climatic changes.

And over the long course of the millennia, thousands of species of animals came and went. You're probably familiar with the names of some of those strange and fascinating creatures: saber-tooth tigers, woolly mammoths, and, of course, the dinosaurs.

Not many people stop to think of it, but one of the things God was doing when he created those species of animals was giving human beings a treasury of subjects to study during our lifetimes. Whole fields of science are devoted to the research and categorization of prehistoric insects and prehistoric marine life. Paleontologists spend decades of challenging and enjoyable work trying to discover whether dinosaurs were smart or stupid, fast or slow, and why they eventually became extinct. What God actually did during those 4.6 billion years was to create the greatest underground science institute/natural history museum of all time.

And don't forget the children. God knew very well when he created the first tyrannosaurus and brontosaurus that little boys and girls would be thrilled by the very thought of them billions of years later. In fact, God might have made the dinosaurs and allowed them to roam the earth for millions of years for *that reason alone.* I can already hear the atheists and evolutionists squealing over that statement, but so what! It's important that we never underestimate God's desire to make us happy and his willingness to do outrageous things to achieve his goal.

But that's not all. We've said over and over again that God doesn't throw away the good things he creates. Well, that applies to prehistoric creatures, too. When I said before that heaven was going to be filled with animals, I meant *filled* with animals—all kinds of animals from all periods of history. There is no reason to believe that in heaven there won't be real, live dinosaurs, not the shellacked skeletons you see in museums.

Heaven is going to be a vast, colorful tapestry of living things. Our God is a God of life, and his home is going to reflect that. Did you ever see the movie *Jurassic Park*? Knowing what we know about God and his love for diversity, why shouldn't it be true that at least part of heaven is going to be like that? When we walk through the woods in heaven, we're going to see friendly lions and monkeys playing with brontosaurs and stegosaurs. When we sail on a boat in the sea in heaven, we're going to marvel at dolphins and seals swimming alongside ichthyosaurs. We're going to be able to lift our eyes to the sky in heaven and watch bluebirds and mockingbirds flying in the air with pterodactyls. It's going to be quite a picture to behold.

Does all this seem too childish and silly to believe? I certainly hope so, because that's a sure sign that it's true. *In order to enter the kingdom of heaven, you have to be like a little child.*[5] Remember that important line from the scriptures? Well, we have to start taking that more literally.

Human beings are never going to understand heaven until they understand a fundamental point about how God's mind works. God is *playful.* Yes, he's serious about his commandments; yes, he can be solemn about the honor and worship due to him; yes, he's demanding about what he expects from us. But with all that, he's still playful. And our capacity to enjoy our life right now, as well as our life in the world to come, is directly tied to our ability to adopt that playful attitude.

Does that mean we can't ever be serious? Of course not. But it means we have to be serious without being gloomy, mature without being stuffy. It means we have to have a childlike openness about everything we do.

It's in this spirit of openness and playfulness that we've tried to paint an exciting picture of heaven so far. Indeed, we've filled paradise with all the things we love on Earth, and many more from the imagination of God. We've included mountains and streams and cities, as well as animals and plants and people. But we've left out one thing.

There's one other creature we haven't discussed yet—and these creatures were around long before human beings and animals came into existence. Chances are they've played an important role in your own life, although you may not have been aware of it. In fact, don't look now, but there's probably one peering right over your shoulder . . .

CHAPTER 7

Our Tour Guides

Wouldn't it be great to go on vacation and have your own personal planner and tour guide? Someone who could assist you in planning your trip, and then show you the best sights to see once you arrive? Someone who could anticipate your every need beforehand and then help facilitate arrangements so that you could get to where you were going quickly, safely, and efficiently?

Wouldn't it be nice to be able to turn to such a guide for help whenever you were having trouble understanding the native language or customs?

And wouldn't it be even better if this personal tour guide knew how to stay in the background and not make a nuisance of himself? After all, you wouldn't want some-one on top of you all the time. Not on *your* vacation.

Well, if something like this is desirable for the trips we take on Earth, don't you think the same would hold true for a trip to heaven? God is the king of all travel agents and heaven is his five-star resort. He knows ex-actly what kind of help we need in order to get to para-dise, and it should come as no surprise that he's arranged to provide each and every one of us with a personal tour guide, of sorts.

Who am I talking about? Who are these heavenly travel assistants? You know them very well—they're called angels.

Angels are pure spiritual beings created by God to assist in carrying out his will. The Bible seems to indicate that there are zillions of them.[1] Their existence is an ab-solute article of faith for every denomination of Chris-tianity. The Islamic religion believes in them too, and so does Judaism.

According to Christian teaching, every single angel is a personal, individual creature that has intelligence and will. Like us, they have their own names. At various mo-ments in time angels have appeared in physical form, but at their core, they are invisible spirits.

To be a pure spirit is something we find hard to fathom. It means that angels don't have material bodies, which in turn means they don't eat, drink, walk, run, pro-create, or die. It does *not* mean, however, that angels can't see, hear, or "know" things. God simply allows them to perform these functions without the aid of bodily senses. In fact, angels are able to know what's going on around them a lot more efficiently and clearly than humans be-cause they don't have to filter everything through optic nerves, neurotransmitters, and brain cells.

The history of the angels is intriguing. We know that they were created by God sometime before human beings. Like us, they were given the power of free will—the abil-ity to choose to do either right or wrong.

We're all familiar with the story of Adam and Eve—how our first parents disobeyed God and were banished from the Garden of Eden. Well, God tested the angels in some mysterious way too. Only the result was a little more dramatic. The Apostle John calls what happened a "war" in heaven.[2] We don't know the details, but there's no denying that something frightening occurred. God gave the angels a command of some sort and not all of them liked it.

One group obeyed without question. Among these "good" angels were a few whom we've come to know over the centuries—Michael, Gabriel, and Raphael.[3]

Another group of angels chose not to obey. These "bad" angels have come to be known as demons. Their "ringleader" has become quite famous as well. His many names ring down through the ages—Satan, Lucifer, Beelzebub, Mephistopheles. But they all really mean the same thing: the devil.[4]

After their act of prideful insurrection, the devil and his band of rebel angels were banished to hell, where, to this day, they continue trying to offend God by winning souls from him. The loyal angels, on the other hand, stayed in heaven and have been assisting God throughout the course of human history. The biblical accounts of this assistance comprise our main body of knowledge about the angels.

We mentioned in the last chapter that the Bible makes frequent mention of animals. Well, it's even more full of great angel stories: an angel was responsible for closing up the Garden of Eden after Adam and Eve were banished; an angel stopped Abraham from slaying his son; an angel announced the conception of John the Baptist, and then the conception and birth of Jesus himself. An angel told Joseph to take Mary and the baby Jesus and flee from Herod into Egypt; an angel served Jesus after he was tempted in the desert; an angel also gave Jesus strength and encouragement during his agony in the Garden. In the Book of Revelation, we see that angels will one day be charged with the duty of destroying the world.[5]

By examining these stories closely, we can see what roles angels play in God's overall plan. For example, it's apparent that angels provide human beings with comfort, both spiritually and physically. They also proclaim the truth. Angels sometimes carry out God's judgment through punishments; and they often act as messengers for God. In fact, the word "angel" in Greek means "messenger."

But the angelic ministry we're most familiar with is that of *guardian*. We said a moment ago that angels could be considered personal tour guides on our trip to heaven. We're able to use that metaphor with some accuracy because the Bible makes it clear that God loves using his angels as instruments to guide us along the path to salvation.

Amazingly, this doctrine of faith is almost universally believed by Jews, Muslims, and Christians. The Catholic tradition is even more explicit, and teaches categorically that each and every human being has a specially appointed guardian angel, whose mission it is to watch over us from the moment we're conceived to the moment we die. (In the Gospel of Matthew, Christ says about children: "See that you do not despise these little ones, for I say to you that their angels in heaven always look upon the face of my heavenly father.")[6]

So what does all this mean for us travelers?

First and foremost it means we're lucky! Not only

do we have a God who gives us full access to himself through prayer; not only do we have a God who gives us his Word in Scripture; not only do we have a God who gives us the rich life of his Church on Earth; but we have a God who is so dedicated to our success that he even provides us with special assistants to help us on our journey to heaven.

These special assistants are also our special friends. We have to remember that the angel who's been assigned to us has a mission to help us. That's what he does for a living![7] If that doesn't make us feel special, nothing will.

Our guardian angels do all sorts of wonderful things for us. They inspire us with creative and virtuous thoughts, they suggest ideas to us that we might not otherwise have had by ourselves, they *tempt* us to do good, they can even intervene in our lives to save us from physical harm.

Of course we have to be careful about what we attribute to angelic intervention. It's easy to slip into superstition, and that's the last thing God wants to happen. We can never be sure when an angel has guided us or protected us in a supernatural way. We may suspect that something miraculous like that has occurred, but very rarely is it ever revealed to us as fact. Those are the kinds of things we won't know for sure till we get to heaven. Someday we'll actually be able to speak to our guardian angel and ask him exactly at which moments in our life he came to our aid—maybe even to our rescue.

For now, though, it's crucial we understand one important point: our angels are *here.* They are here with us *right now.* Because they're spirits we can't know whether they're standing or sitting or hovering nearby. But they are present. In the truest, most objective sense of the word, they are present. And they are focusing their attention on you at this very moment that you are reading these words.

Take a second to reflect on that. Your own personal angel, who was with you when you were a little baby in the crib, and will someday be there at your deathbed, is now watching you read. He's different from other angels. He's got his own special set of characteristics and skills— his own personality, if you will. He's a unique individual, with unique talents and powers that he's used before to help you at various moments in your life.

Exactly which moments were those?

Who can say for sure? But was there ever a time you were feeling particularly depressed, and suddenly a hopeful thought popped into your head? What about a time when you were just about to give in to some temptation, and quite unexpectedly you experienced a burst of spiritual strength? Maybe once you were in the throes of making an agonizing decision, and in a flash all the pieces came together and the answer to your problem became clear. Maybe something even more dramatic happened. Maybe one day you woke up late for work and missed your bus—maybe you spent an hour frantically rushing and cursing, only to find out later that the bus you were trying to catch was involved in a bad accident on the highway.

As we've said, you can never know for sure when you've been the recipient of angelic assistance, but there's a good possibility it's happened to you at some point in your life. Have you ever given that any thought? Have you ever really shown your guardian angel any gratitude for all he has done for you in obedience to God? Have you ever even introduced yourself to him? If not, I have a suggestion for you: Stop being so rude!

You've got a marvelous friend sitting beside you who's been a great companion to you through good times and bad—and you haven't thanked him once. It's time you remedied that situation!

I'm only half joking. You see, angels are not boring, emotionless creatures. We tend to think that way sometimes because it's difficult for us to imagine spirits without bodies. But the Bible tells us explicitly that angels "rejoice."[8] That means they experience feelings of some kind—at least in the figurative sense.

Don't you think they would enjoy it if the person they were guarding and guiding for seventy-odd years at least acknowledged their existence? Don't you think they would appreciate it if the person they were watching over every hour of the day, seven days a week, liked them and maybe even felt affection for them?

Now we have to be careful here. Catholics have always thought it appropriate to cultivate a loving devotion to our guardian angels. Most Protestants, on the other hand, have maintained that it is spiritually dangerous to have "relationships" with any supernatural being other than God Almighty. My point here is simply that it's possible for us to have a more playful attitude toward the angels—just as we have playful attitudes toward other human beings. We are all fellow creatures, after all.

Some spiritual writers have suggested that we even give our angel a name. I know that might sound a little juvenile, but believe me, your angel won't mind. If anything, he'll be gratified to receive some personal attention—finally. I know some people who have been calling their angels by name for years. They don't often do it in public, of course (for fear they might be hauled away in a white van), but they most certainly do it when they're alone. It's a playful way to establish a connection with a very real spiritual being. After all, God loves it when we get outrageous about things that are important to him.

Another important thing we can do is to try to listen more carefully and attentively to our angel, in the event

God wishes to use him to guide us in some matter. God communicates with us in so many marvelous ways. His Holy Spirit sometimes speaks to us directly, sometimes through the words of the Bible, sometimes in a rousing prayer service, sometimes in a powerful sermon, sometimes in music, sometimes through the conversation of friends—and sometimes through angels. But the world we live in is so noisy that the sound of God's voice is often drowned out. If God is going to send one of his angelic tour guides to give us some direction, we have to be ready and willing to hear the message. And sometimes, the only way to do that is to turn off the TV, the radio, the cell phone, and just sit silently and *listen.*

Finally, we can get to know our angels better by utilizing them more. Remember, their God-given mission is to assist us on the way to heaven. They are the tour guides God has provided for us! We should take them up on this more often. There's nothing wrong, for example, with calling on our angels for help when we're in trouble. There's nothing wrong, furthermore, with asking them to communicate with other human beings or other angels on our behalf. The great mystic Padre Pio had an almost childlike faith about the angels. He was so busy with appointments during the day that, in order to save time, he would often tell the people who attended his masses to send their angels to him with their spiritual requests!

It goes without saying that we have to be careful when speaking to our angels in this manner. We certainly don't want to treat them as if they're mere secretaries ("Have your angel call my angel!"). And under no circumstances can we allow our interest in angels to take away from our personal relationship with God.[9] But as I've said so many times in this book, we must not be afraid to be a little lighthearted—especially with our fellow creatures.

You see, no matter how great and wonderful the angels might be, they are still creatures, just like us. The problem is that angels are such marvelous creatures that it's easy for some people—especially religious people—to be overly awed by them. Without even realizing it, they can slip into a "worshipful" frame of mind. After all, angels are immortal, they're powerful, they have the ability to destroy whole cities and worlds, and they can dramatically affect our lives without our even knowing it. Sometimes they can actually seem worthy of adoration. And yet, to even think of worshiping them is diametrically opposed to everything God has in mind for our relationship with them.

Billy Graham, in his book on angels, sums it up well: "If we, the sons of God, would only realize how close His ministering angels are, what calm assurance we could have in facing the cataclysms of life. While we do not place our faith directly in angels, we should place it in the God who rules the angels; then we can have peace."

Angels are sort of like our older brothers. They have authority over us only if our father gives it to them. Yes, they can help us in a thousand different ways; and yes, they can inspire us, guide us, and even save us from harm. But they can do these wondrous things only if God gives them permission.

That's why angels probably find all the press they've been getting lately somewhat embarrassing. The last thing they want to do is be on the receiving end of the credit and public adulation that rightfully belongs to God.

The most compelling reason, however, for treating angels more like equals instead of superiors is that they have to worship their creator in the same way that we do.

Right now, in heaven, tens of millions of them are worshiping the all-powerful, all-knowing, all-good being we call God. At this very minute they are paying homage to the being who created them out of nothing and who set the planets in motion, the being who redeemed the whole world and who keeps all life in existence with the power of a single thought.

Do you know the really incredible thing, though, about this being the angels are worshiping? He is not like the angels. He is *not* pure spirit.

Today, in heaven, that being whom we call God, as the Second Person of the Trinity, wears the form of a *man*.

The dignity that we possess as human beings can never be attained by the angels. When God the Son emptied himself and became one of us in the person of Jesus Christ, as every Christian in the world believes, he forever altered the dynamics of the relationship between angels and men. Angels may indeed be our "older brothers" now, but *we* are the heirs to the kingly throne.

CHAPTER 8

Rest in Peace? NOT!

Okay, so we've made it to this super resort called heaven. We have a good idea what it looks like. We know the kind of shape we're going to be in when we get there. We know who'll be traveling with us, and our angelic tour guides have given us some idea of the native population of the place.

The question for us now is, once we arrive, what are we going to do there? After all, when you visit Australia, you can don your snorkel gear and dive off the Great Barrier Reef; when you visit Pamplona, Spain, in July, you can drink Rioja and run with the bulls; when you visit County Cork in Ireland, you can kiss the Blarney Stone; when you visit New York at Christmastime, you can ice-skate under the great tree, eat a hot, salty pretzel as you stroll down Fifth Avenue, and take a horse-and-carriage ride through Central Park.

But what about heaven? What kind of activities will be at our disposal there?

And here we come to the single biggest obstacle to imagining life in heaven. Not only is it difficult for us to envision what we might do in the afterlife, but we've been so programmed with negative associations that we don't even want to think about it.

People say they believe heaven is a place of incredible happiness, but deep down, I think they're a little afraid it's going to be, well, *boring.*

Since we were children, most of us have pictured heaven as a place where disembodied spirits float around in the clouds all day, playing harps, singing in choirs, and praying . . . forever and ever and ever and ever. That's not a very exciting prospect for anyone.

Then there are the things we *say* about the afterlife, phrases that have become so predominant in our society that they actually turn us off to the idea of heaven. Chief among these is "Rest in peace."

"Rest in peace" is an old, beautiful way of saying good-bye to the people we love. But it's also extremely misunderstood. When you hear it, certain images naturally pop into your head. Sleep, for example —a very, very long sleep. Other words that might come to mind are: sedate, still, unconscious, dark, and quiet.

But this is not what "Rest in peace" means. Rest is not just what we do to refresh our bodies when we get tired from activity; rest is a state we arrive at after we *achieve* something. When a runner finishes a marathon, he comes to a state of rest, which means that he has completed the race successfully, and no longer has to continue running. He may also need a rest, but that's beside the point.

When we speak about deceased people "resting" we are primarily focusing on the first meaning of the word. These people have successfully completed their life's marathon. They have finished the race. They have achieved the purpose for which they were born—to be with God.

The word "peace" also has several meanings. Yes, it can signify quiet inactivity and relaxation, but that's not what we mean when we apply it to the dead. Peace can also mean freedom from anxiety, freedom from stress, freedom from suffering. Peace can mean that we have absolute certainty we are not in danger—that no matter what happens, we are going to be "all right." The very first words Christ uttered to his disciples after he rose from the dead were "Peace be with you." At another time he told them, "I leave you peace, my peace I give you."[1]

Peace was something he bestowed on them. It was a gift that enabled them to do all they had to do without inordinate fear and stress.

Now, do you think the apostles spent their time relaxing and lounging around Palestine? Was Christ himself a sedate, easygoing type of person? Obviously not. In fact, the exact opposite is true.

Christ—the creator and giver of peace—was one of the most energetic human beings who ever lived. In three short years, he crisscrossed Israel performing miracles, challenging authority, chasing moneychangers out of temples, and teaching thousands of people how they should live. In the process, he changed the world forever. Likewise, the apostles, who were the greatest recipients of Christ's peace, ceaselessly worked to spread the Gospel; they traveled the known globe and endured every kind of suffering, from being stoned to being scourged to being shipwrecked.

"Peace," in the Christian understanding, does not mean inactivity. It means freedom from anxiety so that you can be *effectively active*. Thus the words "Rest in peace," carved on so many tombstones and recited in so many religious services, do not mean that the deceased can finally relax after a busy life of work and hardship. They mean that our departed friends and relatives have successfully completed the first stage of their life and have now qualified to take on the challenge of another, more active life in heaven. Even better, during this "second" life, they will be able to accomplish truly great things because they will be completely free from worrying and suffering.

Once we understand this, we will be in a better position to see all the possibilities that are open to us in heaven. It really goes back to what we said at the outset of this travel guide. Our ultimate destination is not static, cloudy, and boring. It is dynamic: filled with activity, pulsating with energy. It is a place of life, not sleep.

When we get to heaven, we won't know what to do first. As someone once said of Paris in the springtime, the only problem will be deciding where to be happiest. Heaven is going to be a vast wonderland of activities, comprising all that nature has to offer, with fascinating possibilities for new sights, new sounds, and new sensations. And as we've seen, there will be an incredible variety of cities to live and play in as well. We'll have instantaneous access to all these places because our bodies will be completely at the service of our minds, and will be able to take us wherever we want to go in a moment.

T. S. Eliot said that human beings should be explorers, no matter what their age. In heaven, we'll get that chance. There will be so much to see and investigate, so much to enjoy—and so much time to do it in. We'll be able to go on sightseeing excursions to a million different countries, cities, planets, galaxies, and universes.

How would you like to take a day trip to Venus? How about a tour of the Andromeda galaxy? How about spending a weekend in ancient Rome (now restored to brand new)? How about a camping outing with the dinosaurs? Don't be afraid to let your imagination run wild! Augustine said, "we will have such bodies that we will be [able to go] *any* place, where and when we want." If you want to understand heaven, you've got to break out of your current pattern of thinking and expand your horizons.

And this applies to the people we're going to see, too. How would you like to go fishing with Ernest Hemingway? Or play catch with Joe DiMaggio? How would you like to discuss literature with Jane Austen, or have Albert Einstein personally explain to you the workings of the universe? How would you like to hear Frank Sinatra sing to you in an intimate cabaret setting? How about taking art lessons from Michelangelo, or piano lessons from Mozart? How about enjoying a cigar and brandy with Winston Churchill? Or playing a round or two of golf with Bobby Jones at Augusta?

Get the idea? As long as the people we just mentioned make it to heaven (and we certainly hope they do), they will be available for us to talk to, work with, get to know better, and become friends with.

All the characters we know from the Bible will be there. We'll be able to meet our first parents, Adam and Eve. We'll be able to talk to Old Testament heroes like Moses and David. We'll be able to "do lunch" with Saints Peter and Paul. We'll be able to sit down under a sprawling tree in the cool of the afternoon with the Blessed Virgin Mary, and ask her what Jesus was like as a little boy.

We'll be able to meet all the famous people we've read about in history, who, hopefully, are there: Socrates and Aristotle, Leonardo da Vinci and Columbus, Washington and Shakespeare, Lincoln and Teddy Roosevelt, Martin Luther King Jr. and Mother Teresa.

Our own ancestors will be there too. How would you like to meet your great-great-great-great-grandfather, and find out all the details of your family history? In heaven, we'll finally have the chance to thank these relatives in person for what they did for us. After all, if it weren't for them, we wouldn't be in heaven.

And as we saw in the last chapter, there will be millions of angels in heaven. We'll be able to interact with these pure spiritual creatures, and ask them at exactly which moments in our life they helped us most. We'll be able to form close friendships with them, learning from them and, perhaps, teaching them, as well.

Best of all, God himself will be there, and we'll be able to glorify him and enjoy his fellowship forever. (But much more on that later!)

Imagine the incredible conversations we'll be able to have with all of these beings. It's a good thing heaven lasts for eternity; we'll need that long just to meet everyone!

Of course, we shouldn't get the idea that heaven is only for fast-paced sightseeing and friendly chatter. There will be plenty of time for the simple pleasures in life too: hiking through the mountains, horseback riding along the shore, taking a brisk walk through the park, reading a really good book by the fireside with a hot cup of tea nearby, enjoying a pleasant meal with your friends.

And there will be so much to learn. Our God is an infinite being. No one could ever fully comprehend all there is to know about him because there's simply too much to take in. Someone once compared it to trying to put all the ocean's water in a sand hole at the beach. It can't be done. God just won't "fit" completely into our minds. That's true now and it will be when we're in heaven. The same can also be said of his creation—we may indeed be able to master vast quantities of information about different aspects of life and nature and people and the universe, but we will never be able to fully grasp it all. The reason is that creation itself is a reflection of God—and both will always remain somewhat unfathomable.

The great news about this is that it will give us the opportunity to study and learn forever. In *Lost Horizon*, by James Hilton, the immortal residents of Shangri-la are free to spend centuries at a time learning new languages, mastering new hobbies, studying new disciplines. Heaven is going to be something like that.

Do you want to take up Greek or Italian? How about the violin or cello? Are you interested in astronomy or physics? Would you like to brush up on your geography, or learn more about history or architecture? Churchill said, "When I get to heaven I mean to spend a considerable portion of my first million years in painting, and so get to the bottom of the subject." Sir Winston was exactly right! In heaven you'll have the time to do all of these things and more. There will be new discoveries around every corner, new subjects to fascinate, interest, and enthrall us everywhere we look.

And let's not forget work.

Work? In heaven? Before I lose you, let me explain. Working in heaven will be more satisfying and more exciting than anything we've ever done in this life. In fact, it will be a key part of what makes us happy for eternity.

First, we have to understand that work is not a human invention. It's from God. Even if we had all the money in the world, we would still need to engage in some form of labor, because that need has been *programmed* into us by our creator.

Go back to the Book of Genesis, when God created the Earth, the water, the sky, the animals, and the human beings, and then rested on the seventh day.[2] Let me ask you a question: What do you think he was taking a "rest" from?

The act of original creation was *work*. God could have chosen to create the world in a nanosecond. All he had to do was snap his fingers and everything we know would have come into existence. But he didn't. Instead, he took his time.

Moreover, when he revealed the story of creation to us in scripture, he made sure to tell us that it was a chronological progression, with a beginning, middle, and end. At the conclusion of the process, he even let us know that he took a day off.

Later on, we see Christ himself working as a humble carpenter. Again, he obviously didn't need to work, he was God. He chose to be a manual laborer. And later still, we learn that St. Paul, the greatest evangelist of all time, flatly refused to live on charity, only accepting the food he was given as payment for his work as a tent maker.[3]

And let's not forget that even in heaven God is, according to St. John, "at work until now."[4]

In all these examples and hundreds more, God is trying to teach us a lesson: work is sacred, work is virtuous, work is holy. It is also deeply satisfying as long as it is meaningful.

John Paul II has written that work "has been taken up in the mystery of the incarnation, and has also been redeemed in a special way."

Does this mean we're going to have "jobs" in heaven?

No one can say for sure. We know that in heaven there won't be a need for many of the goods and services we have here on Earth. For example, there won't be any suffering in heaven, so we won't need hospitals, doctors, nurses, ambulance drivers, therapists, or pharmacists. There won't be any crime in heaven, so we won't need police, lawyers, judges, or wardens. And since no one ever dies in heaven, we won't need any funeral parlors, undertakers, or coroners (thank God!).

If you work at any of the aforementioned jobs, be advised you're going to have to change professions!

On the other hand, there are such things as basic human desires. As long as we are human beings, we'll have the need for beauty, growth, learning, love, and relationships. We need them right now, and we'll need them after we spend our millionth year in heaven. That means that for all eternity, there will be artists, teachers, musicians, and performers.

I'm not saying that if you're an author now, you'll be one in heaven. Or that if you're a singer now, you'll be one in heaven. But you can be sure that some form of human creating will be going on in the afterlife. Books will be written and read, public structures will be built and utilized, works of art will be created and admired, concerts will be performed and attended.

The Reverend James T. O'Connor, in his wonderful book *The Land of the Living*, reaffirms this truth: "The Saints shall work and shall enjoy it, finding in it an outlet for their *heightened creativity,* as well as a means by which they may glorify the Creator."

And remember, we don't have to limit our speculation to merely what we know from our lives here. The raw material humans will have at their disposal in heaven will be of an infinite variety. As we said previously, matter will be totally obedient to our will. Thus artists in heaven will no longer have to restrict themselves to paints, canvases, blocks of marble, or lumps of clay. If they wish to produce something magnificent, they'll have the option of sculpting planets and solar systems! They will be able to share in God's creative powers to a degree never before imagined.

All of this activity constitutes "work." But the difference between work in heaven and the kind that we do now is that our heavenly labor will never be *drudgery*. In heaven we won't need food or money or insurance of any kind, so the work we do will never be forced. Did you ever wonder why some people can perform fifteen hours of intensive labor and still seem refreshed and energized at the end of the day, while others struggle just to make it through the morning? The simple reason is that some people hate their jobs, while others love them.

In heaven, the work we do will seem like play, because we will truly love doing it. At the same time, it will be something that expands us as human beings and expands heaven itself. A better phrase for it might be "active contribution."

One of the keys to finding happiness is to make sure we are constantly growing. No matter how much money we earn, no matter how famous we get, no matter what great things we achieve, it is critical that we have some goal beyond ourselves that we are always trying to reach. That doesn't mean that we shouldn't take relaxing vacations or retire at sixty-five. But it does mean that no matter what our age or financial position, we must always be learning, always expanding, always improving. If we don't, we are doomed to feel dead and empty at the end of each day. This is a law of the universe as immutable as the law of gravity.

It's no accident that God built us this way. He knew that by giving us a psychology that demands expansion, he was providing us with a source of never-ending excitement. When we are in the "mode" of improving, our life is full of possibilities—possibilities for better relationships, better finances, better health, better times.

The work we do in heaven and the growth we achieve will be profoundly fulfilling to us at the very deepest level of our being. The nearest thing we can compare it to is the unbridled joy children feel in anticipation of Christmas or some other future event. Think back for a second to when you were ten or eleven years old. Can you recall a childish dream you had back then? Something you were really looking forward to? Can you remember some happy, carefree fantasy you had about becoming a sports hero, or a movie star, a princess, or president of the United States?

These dreams, when we first visualized them as boys and girls, were intensely exciting to us, not only because they were so grand in scope, but also because we seemed to have so much time to make them come true. When I was in Little League, for example, the dream of playing in the majors was so far off in the future I thought I had forever to hone my skills. But what happened? I got older, and as the years ticked on, I came to the sad realization that I would never be able to achieve such a lofty goal.

Most people have had similar experiences. As we see our time on Earth decreasing, we are forced to "revise" our dreams, to make them less ambitious, less heroic, less exciting. The moment of negative epiphany, when we first realize that our fondest childhood dreams were really only childish fantasies, marks the beginning of our cynical adulthood.

But thankfully, that's not the end of the story.

We've spent all our lives learning that the older we get, the worse things become. We've gotten used to the inevitability of death, suffering, disillusionment, and disappointment. But in heaven, God obliterates these evils forever. Instead of losing time, we gain it; instead of contracting, we expand; instead of slowing down, we speed up; instead of losing our ambition, we get it back tenfold. In heaven, God reverses the dynamic of deterioration that is so characteristic of our lives on Earth.

The reason why Christ continually tells us in the Gospels not to be worried about earthly matters is because God intends to give everything that really matters back to us in the end. Not only will he return the material things that time has so cruelly taken from us—our bodies, our health, our family—but he will restore our most joyful emotional states as well, including our ambition to accomplish great things. By ordaining that our life in paradise be filled with self-improving work and active contribution, God, in a sense, gives us back our dreams. Indeed, he gives us back childhood itself.

The difference is that in heaven, the goals that we set for ourselves will be real, and the time we have to achieve them truly infinite. Instead of youth being "wasted on the young," it will be lavished on the most wise and appreciative of God's creatures—us!

CHAPTER 9

The Vacation That Never Ends

The second day of any vacation is usually the most exciting one for me. All the aggravation of the first day—rushing to the airport, waiting for luggage, getting checked into the hotel, unpacking, and ironing—is done with and you're finally ready to start having fun. There is nothing quite like the thrill of anticipation, and that is what the second day is all about. The week ahead holds unlimited potential for adventure, and each successive day is a challenge of enjoyment.

As you get toward the end of the trip, however, one of two things usually happens. Either a degree of boredom sets in, and you actually begin to look forward to coming home; or you absolutely dread the prospect of returning to "reality." Most times it's this latter feeling that people have. Vacations come too seldom and go much too quickly.

I think we have similar feelings when it comes to heaven. On the one hand, "eternity" seems too good to be true. After all, how could anyone live *forever?* If there's one thing we're absolutely sure of in life, it's that everything and everyone dies. The very idea of a place where death doesn't exist—where the good times keep rolling on forever—is so alien to us that we can't even imagine it.

On the other hand, if we do accept the idea of eternity, how can we be sure it will be eternal happiness? We have trouble seeing how we can be happy for that length of time. After all, human beings get tired of everything—even the good things in life. It's just our nature. I think some people have an unspoken fear that they might indeed enjoy heaven for three or four hundred years, but not much longer than that. Certainly not for a billion years. How could we keep from getting bored out of our wits?

Which brings us to the question of "time"—one of the most intriguing, complex, frustrating, and difficult subjects under the sun.

If you really want to make your head spin, try reading a book on time theory. Scientists have been arguing for years about whether time existed prior to the Big

Bang, or came about as a result of it, whether the universe as a whole exists in time, or rather, with it, whether time is absolute, as Newton believed, or relative, as Einstein asserted, whether there even is such a thing as time, or really only time-space.

Theologians haven't been a whole lot clearer. Oh yes, it's certain that God is eternal, with no beginning and no end, and that he, himself, does not experience time, because his "substance" is changeless. But whether or not he created time *with* the world, or *before* the world, and whether he, in some way, is *in* time now, by virtue of the fact that he became a man, is all very much a mystery.

Thank God we don't have to figure it out here! There have been some marvelous books written on the subject, both from a purely scientific as well as a purely religious perspective. They delve into all the fascinating questions and theories that we can't explore in this little book. What I would like to do here, though, is outline the basics of what Christianity does teach, and discuss how it applies, practically speaking, to our life in heaven.

The first thing we have to get straight is that there will be "time" in heaven—at least in some form. We know that for a fact because we know that heaven is material as well as spiritual. As we've said, there are going to be trees and rivers and cities and human beings in heaven. There's going to be plenty of activity there too. Humans will be moving around, trees will be stirring in the breeze, rivers will be flowing. Thus there will be *changes* in heaven from one moment to the next. Since time is simply the measurement of change, some version of it must exist there.

This is an important point, because there are people who argue that time doesn't exist in heaven—that eternity is really just "awareness," and that there is no "progression of moments" in the afterlife.

Well, that might be the way it is for God and even for the angels, but not for us material creatures. As long as we have bodies that can move, we'll be able to time those movements. As long as we have wrists, we'll be able to wear wristwatches! How we experience time in heaven will certainly be different from how we experience it now, and we'll talk about that in a little while. But as we've seen throughout this book, God is very consistent. He never totally gets rid of anything that's served him well. Time in heaven is going to be recognizable and similar to time on Earth. It might be transformed and renewed—but not destroyed.

The only thing we know for sure will be destroyed in the afterlife is death (and, of course, the activity by which death was brought about—sin).[1] This elimination of death is going to result in a fundamental shift in the way we feel about time. Right now, even if we manage to adopt a positive attitude about aging, we can't help but feel that time is the ultimate villain. No matter how much we try to slow him down, he marches on relentlessly—and forces us to march with him—to a destination that is always the same: deterioration, death, and decay.

It's been said that all stories are tragic, because all stories—if taken far enough—end in death. From that perspective, the happier the story, the sadder it must inevitably turn out. Sometimes, we're acutely aware of the tragedy of life. Other times we manage to keep it in the background of our minds. Either way, the specter of death is always hanging over us in some way. It colors our thinking and taints our experiences in ways we can't quantify.

Anytime something good comes to an end, we feel sadness, not only because that particular pleasure is finished, but because it is a reminder of our own mortality. God makes sure to provide us with plenty of these reminders, because he knows that if he doesn't, we'll be content to live in denial, moving blindly and irresponsibly toward every pleasure, paying little attention to him and the things he has said are important to us. Not only does he allow people and animals we love to die, but he puts other, less traumatic signposts along the way. He allows days to end, seasons of the year to end, vacations to end, meals to end, holidays and family gatherings to end, good books to end. All these things end because God wants to teach us a big lesson: namely, that *we're* going to end one day too—maybe sooner than we think—and he wants us to be fully prepared for that eventuality.

But it won't be like that in heaven. We won't have that oppressive cloud hanging over our heads. It's impossible to repeat enough: *there is no death in heaven.* Christians believe that you are created out of nothingness, that you have one lifetime on earth, that you die only once, you are judged on the basis of that one lifetime, and then live forever afterwards.[2] That's our religion. That's the "good news" of the Gospels. When we get to heaven, one of the most spectacular things about our life there will be the certitude we have that it's not going to end. We'll never again associate the progression of time with proximity to "the end." The good times we have there will thus be untainted and uncolored.

Now while we may understand all this intellectually, and while we may believe it on faith, it's still difficult for us to "feel" it in our gut. Phrases like "life everlasting," "for all eternity," and "forever" are just words to us. Can we really, fully appreciate what they mean? What does it feel like to live forever—to go on a vacation that never ends?

Someone once told me to picture it this way: imagine a long shoreline of beach. Then imagine that a little bird comes along and picks up one single grain of sand from that beach, and flies off with it to a distant land. A million years later, the bird returns, and picks up another grain of sand. He flies off again, for another million years, and then returns. He does the same thing over and over, each time flying off for a million years. Then imagine that the bird does this for every grain of sand on every beach in the entire world. It will take him zillions of years to accomplish his task, but eventually, he will do it. When he does, our *first day* in heaven will not even have dawned.

This kind of fanciful thinking might seem silly to some, but that's the only way we're going to be able to make "forever" real in our minds. If you took five minutes a day to meditate on this one truth, using your own examples and images, I guarantee you'd begin to appreciate the magnitude of the gift God is offering us.

Of course, once we've acknowledged what Christianity teaches about life everlasting, and once we've tried a few times to imagine what that length of time is going to feel like, we've still got the problem of boredom to contend with. How are we going to manage to be happy for a million, a billion, or a zillion years? Won't we run out of things to do?

The best way to deal with this problem, of course, is to simply trust God. After all, if God is so powerful and intelligent that he can create the universe and put the planets in their orbits, then he is certainly smart enough to keep us amused for eternity! But human beings are weak. We want to know *how* God intends to do this.

The reason we're afraid of getting bored with certain pleasures in heaven is because we've already had the experience of getting bored with them on Earth. What we don't realize is that *we've got things reversed*. We try to do fun things in our life now because we want to generate good feelings. When we become bored with something, it's not because we're tired of the good feelings; it's because the specific thing we're doing isn't generating those feelings anymore. So we try other things. They work for a while, and then we tire of them as well.

If we do too much of any thing, we get tired of it. But we never get tired of the feeling that we're trying to produce. Have you ever gotten tired of happiness? Have you ever gotten tired of feeling fulfilled? Have you ever gotten bored with smiling or laughing? Of course not.

In heaven, we won't have to try to produce those feelings artificially. We'll already have them, to the fullest possible extent. We'll have them just by virtue of being with God, as we'll see more fully in the next chapter. Any pleasures we indulge in—and there will be lots—will be icing on the cake. For example, we'll take tremendous pleasure in flying through the air, visiting great cities, playing with animals, exploring the universe, meeting famous people from history, and developing our God-given talents, but we won't need to do any of these things to be happy. So we'll never get deathly bored with them and move on to something else out of sheer desire to satiate a yearning. Happiness will be our *starting point*.

And what about boredom with existence itself — with all that time we'll have on our hands? We've said that in heaven, both human beings and the Earth are going to experience resurrection. They'll be reborn to a new kind of life. Well, the same is going to be true for time — and its resurrection and transformation are going to eliminate any possibility of boredom.

How can we be so sure? God has already given us some powerful clues. We've all seen them before, but we may not have identified them for what they are — glimpses of our life to come.

Have you ever been so deeply involved in your work or in some activity that you lost all track of time? Maybe you were shopping for clothes. Maybe you were playing sports. Maybe you were making love — or reading a good mystery novel. What did the passage of minutes and hours feel like to you at those moments? Didn't the time seem to go very fast? Didn't it fly, as the saying goes?

Sometimes, the opposite occurs. Do you remember sitting in a classroom when you were little, watching the hands on the clock move at a snail's pace toward three o'clock? Didn't it seem to take an eternity for the second hand to move around the dial?

Why does the clock seem to go so fast at some times and so slow at others? And why, at other times, does it stop moving completely?

Have you ever had the experience of standing before a natural wonder of the world like the Grand Canyon or Glacier Bay—spectacles so awesome in scope and breathtaking in beauty that you couldn't feel or think about anything else; when everything in life—including time—ceased to exist, and there was only that vision before you? Have you ever looked into the eyes of the person you loved most in the whole world and felt the same way?

At those special moments, it's hard to tell how much time actually passes. In a very real way, time stands still.

We call those experiences transcendent, because they go beyond all quantifiable limits. If we used a stopwatch to measure them, we'd see that the actual rate of time elapsed was the same for each—sixty seconds per minute, sixty minutes per hour. But that doesn't matter. While the sense of time may have been subjective, the experience was real.

Heaven is going to be like that. The sight of God will be much more heart stopping than any canyon. Therefore our experience of time will be much more transcendent. No one can say for sure whether there will be sixty-minute hours or twenty-four-hour days in heaven. But there *will* be time, and you can be sure we will experience it in a way that precludes boredom. The best way to sum all this up is to go back, once again, to the example of your childhood. That's the key to understanding so much about the afterlife. We've seen how a child in a classroom waits an eternity for his school day to end. But how does that same child feel at the end of the semester, when school lets out and summer vacation begins? How long does the summer seem to that child?

I don't know about you, but when I was a boy, summer vacations were joyously endless. Looking back now, I can't believe they lasted only two months. They seemed to go on forever. To be sure, the days themselves flew by. But that's because I was enjoying myself so much. The scope of the summer itself was vast, the end always so far off in the distance. The reason is that I was doing things that I loved to do—like playing with my friends—and I had no real burdens or responsibilities weighing on my shoulders.

As we get older, the situation often reverses. We get jobs that are not fulfilling and our responsibilities multiply geometrically. The result is that a flip-flop occurs in the way we perceive time. The days themselves go slowly because of boredom and drudgery, and yet, the years seem to pass at the speed of light.

Eternity in heaven is going to be a throwback to when we were children. It will be like summer vacation all over again — or perhaps, the second day of a really great vacation. We'll have no burdens weighing us down, no boredom or frustration, no feelings of pressure — just the thrill of anticipation for all the wonderful years that lie ahead. In this case, though, it really will be an eternity ahead of us, and not just a childish illusion.

CHAPTER 10

The Highlight of the Trip

I've been extraordinarily lucky in the number of European trips I've been able to take, especially to Italy. However, most of these were purely business, and I managed to squeeze in only a few hours here and there for sightseeing. A few years ago, I decided it was time to take a real vacation to Italy. No meetings, no work, no appointments of any kind. I packed the trip with as many "fun" things as I could think of. My wife and I spent the first half week in Rome, visiting all the magnificent churches and museums; then we took the train up to Venice for a few days, where we gondola-ed through the waterways, relaxed in St. Mark's square, and bought Murano glass. From there we headed down to Florence, where we gave our regards to Michelangelo's *David* and haggled with all the gold sellers on the Ponte Vecchio. Then we slowly made our way south, taking several side trips to wonderful medieval hill towns like Assisi and Orvieto. We even managed to visit Naples, where we took the hydrofoil out to the Isle of Capri and rowed through the Blue Grotto. We ended the vacation back in Rome, making a last round at all our favorite cafés and trattorias.

As you might guess, we had a marvelous time. But do you know the best part of the trip? The second-to-last night in Rome, when we arrived back at the hotel after a long day of touring, there was a message waiting for me at the front desk. It read: *Be at the Bronze Doors tomorrow at 7 A.M. You have been invited to attend Mass with the Pope in his private chapel.*

I remembered I had written a letter to the Pope's secretary two months earlier, asking for an audience. But I never dreamed it would actually happen. I had forgotten all about it, and now, reading the note in the lobby of the hotel, I felt a tingling up my spine.

The following morning, when it was still dark, we took a cab to St. Peter's Basilica. It had rained the night before and the stone pavement was still glistening wet. We made our way across the square, past Bernini's fountains, and through the long, curved colonnade, until we arrived at the "Bronze Doors," where we were met by the

Swiss Guard. After going through the appropriate security checks, we were ushered to a waiting room along with a handful of other people, and then up a long, winding staircase, through a courtyard, and into another waiting room, where we removed our coats. Finally, we were escorted into a very small, very plainly decorated room — the private chapel of the Pope.

He was already there, with his back toward us, facing the altar. He was kneeling and praying. I won't go into all the details of the Mass, except to say that it was an experience of a lifetime. This man, who is the head of the entire Catholic Church, and who has the power to influence history as much as any president or world leader, was standing not two feet from me, praying, speaking softly, even making eye contact with me occasionally.

After Mass, we were led out of the chapel and into the Pope's library, where we formed a receiving line, and waited for the pontiff to finish his own private prayer. After about ten torturous minutes, the large wooden doors finally opened and we saw the familiar figure in white. The Pope slowly made his way down the line, saying a word or two to everyone. When he got to me, I stood there, speechless, with a dumb, blank look on my face. By the time I finally gathered my thoughts together and opened my mouth to speak, he had already gone on to the next person, who happened to be my wife. She, of course, had no trouble saying something gracious and appropriate.

But that didn't matter to me. I had met the Pope.

The point is that although my vacation in Italy had many magical moments—visiting the Colosseum, seeing the Sistine Chapel, drinking Chianti in Tuscany, taking a boat trip on the Grand Canal—one stands out above the rest. Meeting the Pope, even though it lasted only a few seconds, was more than just a pleasure. It was a moment of deep fulfillment. On the plane ride back home, *that* was what we talked about most. When we told our friends about the trip, that was the part we saved for last. When we look back on the trip years from now, that will be what we remember as the highlight of our time in Italy. Not because the Pope is so holy or because he's better than others, but simply because he holds a position of leadership in the Church and in the world that deserves deep respect.

We're going to experience something of this kind when we go to heaven.

Throughout this book, we've talked about all the wonderful people we'll meet and the places we'll go in the afterlife. But nothing is going to compare with the thrill of *meeting God*. God is infinitely higher than the Pope or any other created being. Therefore the joy we're going to have when we meet him is going to be infinitely greater than any pleasure we feel meeting some exalted person here on Earth. We all know how much fun it can be to meet celebrities or sports figures. People go to great lengths to get backstage passes to concerts just so they can see their favorite rock stars and ask for autographs. Well, God is the king of all celebrities. He's been famous for over a million years. He's the greatest artist who ever lived. He's a world champion fighter who's never lost a bout. And he wrote the Bible, which makes him the number one internationally bestselling author of all time.

But God is even more than that.

Scripture doesn't just say that God is the creator of beauty, power, truth, and life. It says that he *is* beauty, power, truth, and life.[1] That's a difficult concept to understand. It means that when we see material objects on Earth that possess those characteristics, they are really only reflecting different qualities of God. You might say that they're like photographs of God from different angles. The theological explanation is that God is so great, none of his creations can fully reflect him. Instead, they each reflect a small part of him. Some created objects reflect beauty, others love, others truth—all to varying degrees and in different combinations.

The question is, if we can experience joy by looking

at mere reflections, what will the real thing do to us when we finally encounter it?

Let me put it another way. People get tongue-tied and nervous when they meet a beautiful person of the opposite sex. How do you think it's going to feel when we meet the *source* of all beauty? People are intimidated when they see the president of the United States, standing with all his Secret Service men around him, the leader of the most powerful country in the world. How do you think it's going to feel when we meet the *source* of all power? People are impressed when they meet someone very smart—a great doctor or scientist or professor. Imagine how it's going to feel when we meet the *source* of all knowledge.

Throughout this book we've talked about all the marvelous pleasures we're going to enjoy in heaven. But there's an important distinction we really haven't made between the fleeting, passing joy of "pleasure," and the deep, abiding joy of true "happiness." We're going to experience that in heaven too, and its primary source will be seeing God.

For centuries, theologians have tried to describe what this experience of seeing God, face to face, will be like. They even have a name for it: beatific vision.

They've said that this beatific vision is going to be

the most joyful, exciting, and profoundly satisfying emotional experience human beings will ever have. They've said that it will give us a feeling of supreme happiness; that when we look at God, it will be impossible for us to ever be sad, upset, or depressed again. In fact, the beatific vision is so powerful that theologians have argued if God himself didn't protect us, our souls and bodies would be annihilated just from being in his presence.

How could it hurt us to look at our creator? Think of the sunlight. We love being outdoors in the summertime, going to the beach, playing sports, sitting and reading under a tree. But we would never think of looking directly at the sun for more than a few seconds. If we did, our optic nerves would burn to a crisp and we'd go blind. Well, God *created* the sun. He's the source of its power. It makes sense that he'd be "too much" for us to handle.

In fact, anytime anyone in history has purported to experience a vision of God, they have said they were "overcome" or "overwhelmed." Christian mystics often use the word *ecstasy* to describe the phenomenon. Whatever the terminology, it signifies something pretty powerful. St. Paul was struck blind on the road to Damascus. Thomas Aquinas, after being given a mere glimpse of God while praying, was practically paralyzed. "I can do no more," he said. "Such things have been revealed to me that all that I have written seems to me as so much straw."

In heaven, we know that God will have to find some way to protect us from his awesome power, because he intends to reveal himself to us much more clearly than he has to anyone in the Bible or in the Church. He intends to give us the ability to look him squarely in the face, without anything in between, and experience fully all the love and happiness our souls can handle.

And by the way, the amount of that happiness will be different for each of us. We've said before that heaven is a place of supreme joy, but it's also true that the *level* of joy we experience there is going to be determined by what we do in *this* life. A person whose faith in God has burned brightly through all of life's trials, who has prayed unceasingly, who has patiently borne sufferings and led a holy, selfless, sacrificial existence, is going to be given a greater reward than someone who just made it into heaven by the skin of his teeth!

Now you might wonder how someone in heaven can be given a "lesser" amount of happiness, and yet still be perfectly, supremely happy, and feel just as "fulfilled," in fact, as a person who receives more. Therese of Lisieux, in her book *Diary of a Soul,* used a wonderful metaphor to illustrate this paradox. She described how her sister took two different-size glasses—one tall, one tiny—and filled them both to the top with water. Then she asked, "Which one is more full?" Obviously, both were equally full, though they differed in their capacity to hold water. The same is true for us. In heaven, there will be great, magnificent saints—the tall glasses, if you will—into whose souls God is going to pour incredible amounts of honor, glory, and happiness. Then there are going to be saints who are not quite as great, whose lives on Earth were not as filled with faith and love, but who, nevertheless, received salvation from the Lord. They will be like the small glasses; and while they, too, will be filled to the brim with as much happiness and honor as they can stand, they will not have the same capacity for happiness as some of their brother and sister saints. When we talk about the different "rewards" God is going to give each of us after we die, we are really talking about this capacity to be filled up by God. The good news is that there's still time for each of us to decide what our heavenly capacity for joy is going to be—there's still time to blow the glass out, stretch it and shape it to be what we want.

No matter what level of joy we ultimately receive, however, the bottom line is that the sight of God is going to make us happy. The problem is that while we may understand, intellectually, that the beatific vision will give us extraordinary joy, we don't necessarily feel it, deep in our gut. After all, it's a little difficult to warm up to the idea of a being the very sight of whom can destroy us! And the phrase "beatific vision" itself is so abstract and theological, it's hard for us to get enthusiastic about it. Luckily for us, God understands how our minds work. After all, he invented psychology. He knows how difficult it is for us to connect emotionally with a spirit we can neither see nor touch. So he gave us a great gift. Two thousand years ago, God decided to make it easy for his creatures to know him personally. He did this in the most surprising way: he became one of us.[2]

Everyone knows the story of the first Christmas, how a child was born to Mary in a stable in Bethlehem, and how angels proclaimed to shepherds in the field that a savior had come into the world. As Christians, we believe that God himself took on a human form so that he could personally experience all the suffering in the world, and so he could make up for the sins of our first parents, Adam and Eve, and make it possible for our sins to be forgiven, as well.

Simply put, Christians believe that Jesus is God, and God the Son is Jesus. We said earlier in this book that God is actually three "persons" in one—Father, Son, and Holy Spirit. Christians hold that Jesus is the second person of that Holy Trinity, and that he became human all those years ago and retains his human nature today, in heaven.

This is a critical point. If we really want to understand how wonderful it's going to be to meet God, we first have to get clear in our minds that we won't be just meeting a spirit. We'll be meeting a *man*. When we arrive in heaven, we are not going to see God just floating around in the clouds. God the Son—the second person of the triune God—is going to be walking around on the ground. The experience of the beatific vision will thus be as real and as physical as everything else we've discussed in this book.

The God we're all going to meet after we die is the very same carpenter who lived in Nazareth all those years ago. He's the same miracle worker who "made lame beggars walk and blind men see," the same man who raised the little girl from the dead. He bears the very same wounds he received the day he was crucified. He has the same hair, nose, eyes, and hands as the man who appeared to the apostles on Easter Sunday morning. There's nothing anywhere in scripture to suggest otherwise.

I know it's strange to picture things this way, but it's really what all of Christianity comes down to. In heaven, God the Son is going to be walking, talking, laughing, and enjoying the whole experience right along with us.

If you want a good idea of what our interaction with God is going to be like in heaven, just turn to John 21, and you'll read one of the nicest and most charming scenes in the whole Bible. It takes place after Christ has risen from the dead and has his glorified body—the same one we will see in heaven. The apostles are out fishing one morning, and suddenly they see him on the shore:

"Just as day was breaking, Jesus stood on the beach. . . . When [the apostles] got out on land, they saw a charcoal fire there with fish lying on it, and bread . . . Jesus said to them, 'Come and have breakfast.' "[3]

Christ could have simply appeared to his followers indoors (as he had on other occasions), but instead, he chose to do something more pleasant, something more human, something more fun. He decided to fix them some breakfast outside. God the Son actually prepared a cookout on the beach, complete with barbecued fish! That's the setting he chose for one of his major post-resurrection appearances.

And *that's* how it's going to be in heaven. That's the kind of relationship we're going to have with Christ. Because of that, it will be all the more easy to love him, in a human way.

Everything God did as Jesus Christ was calculated to bring him closer to us. By becoming a little baby, God made it easy for us to approach him. (What's less intimidating than an infant?) When God became a humble carpenter, instead of someone rich and famous, he was making it easier for us to relate to him. When God chose to suffer an excruciatingly painful death, he was making it easier for us to empathize with him. When God rose from the dead on Easter Sunday, and opened the gates of heaven for the rest of us who will die, he was making it easier for us to be grateful to him.

The incarnation (God becoming Man) wasn't only an act of goodness on God's part, it was a stroke of genius! On that first Christmas Day, God jumped headlong into the mix of human experience. He reached down from heaven and "got his hands dirty," so to speak. In one brilliant stroke, he demolished forever the idea of a distant, abstract, invisible creator.

What does all this mean in terms of our life in the world to come? Often Christians talk about the need to develop a "personal relationship" with Christ. In heaven, that relationship will flourish beyond our wildest imagination. When God welcomes us to paradise, he's not just going to shake our hands or give us an autograph, like celebrities do here on Earth. He's going to spend "quality time" with us. We'll be able to talk to him, just like we talk to our friends and family now. We'll hear his voice, and he'll hear ours. We'll be able to look right into his eyes when we're speaking to him. And when we worship him, it won't be like simply going to church on Sunday morning (although I'm sure there will be something like that in heaven too). Many of the prayers we say in heaven may be simple conversations in which we thank God to his face for all the good things he has done for us.

Another thing that's going to happen is that God will answer all the questions we have about our life on Earth. Everyone has unanswered questions: big ones like why was I born? What is the meaning of my existence? What is the purpose of suffering? And smaller ones about the painful events of our life: Why did my mother die when I was thirteen? Why was I crippled in that accident? Why did my father get Alzheimer's? Why wasn't I able to have children? Why was I so depressed and so alone for so long?

Sometimes our questions are of a less traumatic nature: Why didn't I get that job I wanted so much? Why did my life go in this direction instead of the direction I had originally planned? Why didn't this or that relationship work out?

Whatever our questions may be, the fact is that they need to be answered. In heaven, God is going to address every single one of them. "On that day," the Gospel of John says, "there will be no more questions."[4]

You might say God is going to take us on a personal tour of sorts. Not a tour of heaven—but of our own lives. He's going to show us every detail of our earthly existence, from our birth to our death, taking us through all the crazy turns and dips in the road, all the letdowns, all the disappointments, all the successes, all the failures, all the triumphs. This is not to be confused with the Final

Judgment or with the Catholic doctrine of purgatory. What I'm referring to here is the fact that God intends to reveal to us his grand plan for our lives, and how all the events we've experienced—even the tragic ones—somehow fit into that plan.[5] You've heard the expression, "everything happens for a reason." In heaven, we're going to find out what those reasons are. We're going to see how all of the pieces of the puzzle fit together.

It's impossible for us to do that now, for the simple reason that we live in "time." Human beings have a past, present, and future. We experience life as a series of progressing moments, and we can never know for sure what the next moment will bring.

It's not like that for God. God stands outside of time. When he looks down from heaven at John Smith's life, he doesn't just see John the way he is now. He sees all of John's life, from beginning to end. It's as if he's looking at a page titled *John*. He can look up at the top of the page and see John's birth, he can look at the middle of the page and see John getting married, and he can scroll all the way down to the bottom of the page and see John dying in the hospital with his grandchildren around him. He sees it all in one glance.

God sees all of the choices we're going to make in our lives, and all the results of those choices. He sees the mistakes, the sins, the screw-ups. He sees everything we're going to do, and he sees it all ahead of time. In order to accomplish his will he takes all these choices and arranges them in such a way that his plan is ultimately achieved. Theologians call this *Providence*.

How God is able to reconcile his providence with our free will is one of the great mysteries of our faith. We know that when something "bad" happens, God allows it, but that he also arranges things in such a way that "good" will eventually come out of it. In heaven, God will at last show us how he managed to do this, and what specific good things he brought about. We'll find out why that person we loved so much died so young; why those girls in the news story were brutally raped and murdered; why that little boy down the block is autistic—why God allowed all these horrible things to occur, and how he found a way to use them to accomplish some greater good.

God rarely tells us the reasons why he permits such tragedies. Usually, he asks us to rely on him and trust in his judgment. His purpose, always, is to draw us closer to him. Sometimes this happens right away; sometimes it takes us years, especially after the death of someone very close. Unfortunately we won't know the answer to every "why" question until we're with God in heaven.

Now, we shouldn't be afraid that God is going to force us to relive the painful memories we have of life on earth. Not at all. We're not going to begin our stay in paradise by crying! Christianity teaches that our memories in heaven are going to be clearer and more vivid than ever before, but we won't look back at any of them with sadness. We'll remember even the tragic ones with joy, because God will be right beside us and he'll show us how they helped to lead us, in some way, to heaven.[6]

Nor should we get the idea that this tour of our lives is a mere rehashing of all the negative things that have happened to us. God intends to show us the results of our good choices as well. For every time we do something in accordance with God's will, it sets off a chain reaction of good actions. Not that these consequences are always pleasurable to experience. On the contrary, the choices we make in obedience to God's will often lead to a series of persecutions for us. But ultimately, they always add up to something good.

The Frank Capra film *It's a Wonderful Life* illustrates this truth perfectly. In the movie, an angel shows a small-town man named George Bailey what the world would be like if he had never been born. There's a scene toward the end of the picture when the angel takes George to a cemetery and shows him the grave of his younger brother, Harry, whose life George had saved when they were little boys. George reacts angrily when he sees his brother's name on the tombstone, yelling, "That's a lie. Harry Bailey went to war and won the Congressional Medal of

Honor. He saved the lives of every man on his ship." The
angel calmly responds: "Every man on that ship died.
Harry wasn't there to save *them* because *you* weren't
there to save Harry . . . Strange, isn't it? Each man's life
touches so many other lives, and when he isn't around, he
leaves an awful hole."

No act of goodness ever terminates with the end of
the action itself. It goes on in a long, long chain. The same
is true for our prayers. No prayer, no matter how small, is
ever uttered without result. God always answers it in
some way. Maybe not in the way that you want, maybe
not in the way you hope, but always in the way you *need*—
always in the way that is best for the person you're praying for.

In heaven, God is going to reveal to us the consequences of all of our actions and all of our prayers.[7] He's
going to show us the millions of invisible chains that have
stretched out through the ages, connecting stranger to
stranger, event to event, generation to generation. By the
end of this grand tour of our lives, we are going to have a
much fuller, richer, and truer understanding of the impact
we had on those around us—and on the whole world.
That alone would be enough to make this the trip of a lifetime.

CHAPTER 11

A Heavenly Makeover

Up to this point, we haven't really discussed how heaven impacts our lives *now*. Yet, this subject is deeply tied in to the whole Christian doctrine of the afterlife. In fact, it has a lot to do with a key belief held by all Christian denominations: namely, that each and every human being is *special* in the eyes of God.

Why is it so important that we are special?

Let's once again make a comparison with taking a trip. Why do you think people like traveling first class? Is it just because you can board the plane early, or because you have extra "legroom"? Because the flight attendants ply you with food and drink, or because there are shorter lines at the bathroom?

These may all be good reasons, but there's something else, too. Being in an upscale environment, whether it's in a plane, train, cruise ship, or restaurant, gives us the feeling that we have great value—that we are *somebody*. After all, why else would we be treated so well by total strangers?

The same is true for fancy spas, where people spend their days getting manicures, pedicures, makeovers, and soothing massages. These activities are certainly relaxing, but one of the main reasons for their popularity is that they make us feel so special and pampered.

Unfortunately, this desire we have to feel special is something that can easily get out of hand. In fact, it can be very dangerous to us, spiritually, if it translates into a need to feel that we are "better" than the next person. "I drive a Mercedes, own a house in a prestigious neighborhood, wear the best designer-brand clothes, send my kids to the best schools, eat at the chicest restaurants; *therefore,* I must be of greater value than this other fellow, who doesn't have the first clue about the 'finer things in life.' "

Just as people can get addicted to drugs, they can also become addicted to "status." If you get caught in this trap, watch out. Life can quickly deteriorate into a silly form of competition for goods and services that ultimately mean nothing. The end result, if not corrected soon

enough, is an unhappy, dissatisfied life, full of petty jeal-
ousies and shallow relationships.

If you manage to avoid this distorted way of thinking, however, there is something very good and even holy
about wanting to feel special. Like all basic human needs,
the need for significance comes directly from God—he
placed that desire inside of us.

When God created you and me, he didn't give us just
physical fingerprints. He gave us *spiritual fingerprints* as
well.[1] What this means is that every single human being is
radically unique. Of all the billions of people who have in-
habited this planet, *you* have been given some trait, skill,
or characteristic that no one else has ever possessed.

How can we explain this in theological terms? Well,
we said earlier that God is an "infinite" being and that
every material object under the sun reflects him in some
way. The same thing is true of us. We all have within us
some special quality that reflects God differently and more
perfectly than anyone else.

This concept of "reflecting God" doesn't necessarily
have to do with holiness. There may not be anything
about you more virtuous than, say, the apostles. But you
can be sure that, in some aspect of your character, you *are*
superior to them—at least potentially. It may only mean
that you can sing better, or paint better, or have a better
sense of humor, or that you are more intelligent when it

comes to analyzing things. Whatever your special gifts, it is a fact that you have the God-given ability to do certain things that neither they nor anyone else ever could.

The same is true when you compare yourself to any of the illustrious personalities in history. Your own particular skill set and combination of personality traits is different from those of Napoleon, Caesar, Joan of Arc, George Washington, etcetera, and in some way, potentially greater. Everyone in life has been given the gift to be special. This may sound like a cliché, but it is true in the deepest sense. Whether you are the most powerful monarch or the feeblest invalid, there is something about you that is utterly exciting and unique in God's eyes. The problem is that many of us never find out what our "specialty" is.

We can go our whole lives completely unaware that we are *like* God in some way that no one else is. This isn't necessarily our fault. Sometimes a person's special abilities are hidden behind a seemingly impenetrable wall of disability, autism, or old age. God may have X-ray vision and the ability to see through to that individual's greatness, but we don't have that power, and sometimes we fail to realize that these human beings are just as valuable as us.

Thankfully, this isn't the case in heaven. As we've seen, when we experience the resurrection, we enter paradise as our best, truest selves—with our potential fully realized. You might say that our spiritual fingerprints become even more "defined." Even if we don't develop all our gifts in this life, God gives them back to us, many times over, in the next.

This is something of a habit with God. He loves giving things back to us after he has magnified and transformed them. He asks us to give selflessly to help the poor, for instance, and then gives us back an infinitely richer feeling of self-satisfaction. He asks us to sacrifice our time, money, and sometimes our sanity for our children, and then gives us back the much greater joy of seeing them grow up. He asks us to live our lives for the sake of the Kingdom of Heaven, and then gives us what can be a marvelously exciting life *here*.

This last observation—about life on Earth—is something we need to spend some time on, because it's what critics of heaven object to most. These folks believe that the very idea of heaven is destructive because it makes people place all their hopes and dreams in the next life, and forget about *this* one. According to this way of thinking, people who have a strong faith in heaven are more apt to settle for unsatisfying, unfulfilled lives now, because of their belief that they will be "compensated" with a greater reward after they die. Thus, heaven actually stifles the human spirit; it saps creativity, dulls the love of adventure, and ultimately, devalues our lives.

Can this really be so?

Absolutely not! In fact, the opposite is true. When you look back at the long span of human history, it's very obvious that many of the people who made the greatest impact on civilization believed in God. The most notable artists, musicians, explorers, political leaders, monarchs, military men, writers, scientists, and reformers of the past all had faith in the life to come. Not all of these people were "good," of course; in fact, some had very distorted ideas about God and actually used their religion to justify their wicked lives. But whether these historic characters were sinners or saints, their belief in the afterlife certainly didn't stifle their activities in this world.

Why is this the case? Simply because faith in God and heaven makes you *more* interested in what you do in this life—not less. People who have faith know that they are destined for more than just the grave, so they are aware that how they act now has importance beyond the "day to day."

Christians, especially, know that the funeral is not the end of the story. We know we are meant for eternity. Therefore, we know we possess an inherent value and dignity just by being human. And since our fellow human beings have the same value and the same dignity—whatever their situation or physical condition—we have an obligation to care for them and treat them as brothers and sisters. Moreover, when we see injustices being committed against them, we have the responsibility to intercede on their behalf.

In addition to all this, people who believe in heaven know that what we do in this life affects the next. Someday—maybe sooner than we think—we are going to be asked to give an accounting of ourselves—how we lived, what things were important to us, how generous we were, how frequently we obeyed or disobeyed God. In a word, we're going to be judged.

True believers, therefore, are *intensely* interested in this life. They may not always live up to their beliefs, but you can be sure that they won't be sitting around doing nothing, waiting for God to bring them to heaven. They will be as active and energetic as they can in this world.

It comes down once again to what we just said about being special. If you really understand what Christianity teaches about the human person—that we are destined for eternity, that we are loved by God, that we are radically unique—then you will have no trouble grasping why it is a moral imperative for us to do our best to live outstanding lives here on Earth—outstanding moral lives, outstanding social lives, outstanding physical lives. Only by reaching for outstanding levels in everything we do can we hope to discover God's unique and special plan for our life.

Of course we know it's not always easy to do this. It's hard work to constantly try to "improve" ourselves. It's so much simpler to take the path of least resistance. The result of this laxity, however, is that our unique talents often stay buried for long periods. As we noted before, we can easily become hooked on "status" as a substitute for genuine significance, and spend our lives striving to obtain the mere illusion of being special.

But it doesn't have to be this way. God gives us the need to feel special, but he also gives us the *ability*. "I have come," Christ said, "so that you may have life, and have it abundantly."[2] He wasn't referring only to life in heaven when he said this. He was referring to the abundant, overflowing, outstanding, and heroic life he wants all of us to have *now*.

If you have any question in your mind about the importance of *now*, just open the New Testament. Throughout the pages of the Gospels, Christ goes back and forth between describing heaven as a place of the future and as something we can experience—to some degree—in the present. This is a point atheists always seem to miss. They try to paint Christianity as being very gloomy and depressing and death-centered. They forget that Christ himself was constantly saying things like "the Kingdom of Heaven is upon us."[3]

How can heaven be "upon us"? Christianity teaches that while heaven is a very real, concrete place—a place of the future—it also has the power to mysteriously "break into" this world. This point is illustrated beautifully by a strange, almost surreal event related by the Gospel writers. It is an event that, properly understood, shows the great potential for growth that we all have.

One night soon before his crucifixion, Jesus took three of his closest disciples—Peter, John, and James—up a mountainside to pray. As he began to speak to his Father in heaven, his face suddenly changed and became very bright. His clothes turned "dazzling white" and luminous. Out of nowhere, two Old Testament figures appeared beside him and began speaking to him about his impending death. A cloud then covered the hilltop, and the voice of God came from it, saying, "This is my beloved Son, in whom I am well pleased—Listen to Him." Suddenly the cloud vanished and it was dark again, and the disciples were alone with Jesus on the hilltop.[4]

The apostles, naturally, were frightened by all this. They didn't understand what had happened. What they actually witnessed was heaven coming down to Earth; what they saw was Christ as he really was, in all his heavenly glory.

This event has come to be known as the "Transfiguration," because Christ was transformed, bodily, before the eyes of his disciples. During all the time he had previously spent with them—even while performing great miracles—he looked, sounded, and acted like a normal human being. But in this one instance, he chose to reveal his awesome divinity. What was his reason for doing this?

Undoubtedly there are many theological explanations. One is simply that he wanted to prepare his apostles for the crucifixion. He knew it would shake their faith to see him die, so he wished to give them something beforehand to strengthen and sustain them.

But there is another lesson the Transfiguration has to offer. And it applies to human beings of any era, generation, or age group.

When Christ was transfigured on that little mountaintop in Judea, he wasn't only revealing his glory—he was revealing *ours*, as well. In demonstrating his divinity to the apostles, he was also showing us the spiritual majesty we all possess, since we are all made in the image and likeness of God. What Christ was essentially doing was giving us a practical demonstration of the potential humans have to lead dazzling, luminous, glorious lives.

We described earlier in this book how Christ rose from the dead and appeared to his disciples on Easter Sunday; how he exhibited amazingly powerful qualities that give us a glimpse of what we will be like in heaven. But Christ wasn't content to wait till after his resurrection to manifest these qualities. He very deliberately transfigured himself *before* his death. In doing so, he was sending us a message: *we don't have to wait* till we are dead to experience the power and glory of heaven. By virtue of the fact that we have immortal souls, we have the power to live "transfigured" lives right here on earth.

How can we do that?

I'm afraid that's the subject for another book. But I'll give you a clue—it involves a whole new way of looking at yourself and your potential, a new conviction you must have about your God-given ability to transform your life—not just by your own disciplined efforts, but through the assistance of a God who is ready to help you the moment you ask him.

It involves living your faith to the max, and exercising the true meaning of love in your life, which means sacrificing your desires for the sake of others. It involves dedicating yourself—no matter how "bad" you may have it—to helping alleviate the suffering of others. It involves daring to do great things in the eyes of God, even if you're restricted to a hospital bed.

In a word, it means catching the "vision" of the Transfiguration and applying it to your own life.

Let me give you one example. I have a good friend

who recently beat cancer. It was a long and grueling process, with plenty of good days and bad, full of suffering, both emotional and physical. But miraculously, she triumphed. My friend was a relatively successful person before she contracted the disease, but now, she is a veritable powerhouse of activity. Not only is she thrilled about her life, but she is making bold, exciting moves that she would never have dreamed of making several years ago. Why? Because she faced death with courage and faith, realized God was going to be with her no matter what the outcome, and made the best of a tragic situation. As it turns out, God has other plans for her. Now that she is in remission she has a new lease on life. Only it's a *new kind* of life. A life unfettered by the paralyzing fear of death—a life of taking more chances and striving for greater things. It's not just about money or status, it's about doing things that are really valuable and accomplishing things that are truly worthwhile.

You see, believing in heaven never restricts you. It frees you and liberates your life. It teaches you that you are not here by chance, that you have the power to be master of your fate, that God has heroic plans for you, and that nothing—nothing except turning away from God—can ever really hurt you.

Terms like *heroic* and *glorious* may seem exaggerated to some, but I assure you, they are not. Whether you are the CEO of a billion-dollar corporation, a teenager plagued by self-doubt and insecurities, an older man ravaged by disease, a working woman trying to balance her family life and career, a drug addict who's hit rock bottom, an overworked lawyer, or an underappreciated mom—God has mighty plans for you, if you'll only listen to him.

God's goal, always, is to take whatever life you happen to be born into, or whatever life you happen to make for yourself, and transform it into something greater, grander and more awesome.

How this "greatness" will manifest itself is anyone's guess. It might be that you're destined to save someone's life in a fire. It might be that you're going to make millions of dollars and give it away to charity. It might be that your daughter will someday find a cure for cancer. It might be that in your old age you'll be the dispenser of life-saving wisdom to your grandchildren. It might be that when you finally receive news that you have a terminal disease, you'll face death with such heroism and good humor that the people around you all remember your faith and are strengthened by your courage till their own dying day.

The point is, whether your life is transfigured by "big" or "small" things is totally unimportant. In God's eyes, all transfigurations are glorious. Your family and friends may not even realize that there's been a change in you, initially. And you may never get famous by the world's standards. But God, who sees everything you do—even those things that are hidden from everyone else—will recognize that you have started down the road to greatness that he has planned for you from all eternity.

The gift you'll get in return for your efforts is nothing less than a foretaste of heaven. You'll actually begin to experience the happiness of heaven right now—no matter what your situation. This obviously doesn't mean that you'll get to see your deceased friends and relatives just yet, but you will be given a tremendous sense of certitude that they are alive and waiting for you on the other side. And while it's virtually certain that you will still have to face more suffering and death in years to come, you will also be given supernatural levels of strength and courage to get you through *anything*. And while you won't get to see God, face to face, in this life, your faith in him will grow by leaps and bounds, until you are more certain of his existence than you are of your own. Indeed, your faith will be indestructible—whether you are standing in the shadow of the cross, or in the brilliant light of the Transfiguration.

Most importantly, you'll be given a deep feeling of inner peace—the kind of peace that comes from knowing your life has meaning and purpose; the kind of peace that comes from knowing you are meant to live forever—the kind of peace that comes only from heaven.

It's ironic that people today spend thousands of hours at the gym or the spa trying to transform their bodies. They want so desperately to shape up, look attractive, and feel good about themselves. They know how important it is to eat right and stay healthy so they can prevent serious physical problems from occurring later on. And yet, the same thing can't be said when it comes to caring for our souls. Very few of us go for "spiritual makeovers" nearly as often as we should.

The all-important question you have to ask yourself as you contemplate the marvels of heaven is this: Why?

Why wait till you are faced with the news of a terminal illness before transforming your life? Why must it take something traumatic and frightening to cause you to finally turn your life around? And why wait till you are dead to experience the joys of heaven—when many of them are available to you right this second?

Why not transfigure your life now?

CHAPTER 12

Your Ticket to Heaven

Now that we've come to the end of this little book, there's only one more question left for us to deal with: Where do we sign up? How can we get our ticket to heaven?

After all, how much would you pay for a ticket to a place like this—a place where you're going to have life everlasting, life with your family and friends, life without suffering, life as a superbeing in a superworld? What would you do in order to gain entry into this community?

Would you endure a terrible illness, for example? Would you be pleasant to the person at work who's so hard to deal with? Would you forgive that family member who offended you all those years ago? Would you put your spouse's interests above your own? Would you go to church once a week?

How about accepting the death of your father, or mother, or sister, or even your son, with faith? Would you grin and bear a period of unemployment? Would you fight your way through depressing money problems, without losing hope and becoming bitter? Would you be able to face your own old age and death with bravery and even cheerfulness?

I don't know about you, but as I've learned more about heaven, my willingness to endure more suffering in this life has also increased. There were times when I remember complaining about every little misfortune I encountered. But as I became more committed to my faith and grew to understand what God was planning to give me, my attitude changed. My belief in the "eternal" helped me to accept many of the sacrifices and hardships of the "temporal."

For when we try to view things through the lens of eternity, the problems and turmoil of our present lives really don't seem quite so big. I'm not belittling suffering in any way, but I am saying that no matter how intense that suffering is, it doesn't compare to the happiness that awaits us.[1] If God is willing to give us all that, what can't we at least try to endure, for his sake?

It's natural for people to question God, to doubt

God—or even to rail against God—after they have suffered a loss. But what we must always try to remember is that God is primarily concerned with one thing: whether or not we make it to heaven. Next to that awesome question, everything else means nothing. If you die at ten years old in an automobile accident, but go to heaven, then you had a successful life. If you die peacefully in your sleep at ninety, rich and powerful in the eyes of the world, but go to hell, then your life was a wasted tragedy. "What does it profit you," Christ asked, "to gain the whole world but suffer the loss of your soul?"[2] We don't always see the truth of this, but God does. When we go to a funeral, or see someone in the street who is crippled or mentally retarded, we torture ourselves by asking all kinds of questions about how different or better that person's life could have been, or why God was so "unfair." But we rarely ask the one question that really counts: Is that person going to heaven? That's the only thing God cares about. That's the lens through which he views our lives.

Now let me ask you another question. Let's say you were going on vacation to Hawaii, and on the day of the trip you went to the airport, stepped up to the ticket counter, and found out that someone had already purchased the ticket for you. In fact, not only had the airline ticket been bought, but the entire package was yours for free—transfers, hotels, helicopter rides, day trips, everything! All you had to do was follow the signs to your gate, and board the plane. How surprised and happy would you be?

Well, that's exactly what God has done for us. He's already purchased our tickets to heaven.

That's the whole meaning of the crucifixion. Before Christ died on the cross and rose from the dead, no one was *allowed* into heaven. From the time our first parents got themselves tossed out of the Garden of Eden for blatantly disobeying God, human beings were denied access to paradise. God himself had to become a man and act in perfect obedience to the will of the Father to make up for Adam and Eve's sin and throw open the doors to heaven once again. When Christ rose from the dead on Easter Sunday, all the souls of the faithfully departed who lived in antiquity were finally allowed to enter heaven with him.[3]

We're allowed to go in too. That's why Easter is such a joyous feast. It's the celebration of the reopening of heaven. All we have to do is *follow the signs to the gate*.

But how, exactly, do we do that?

Unfortunately, this is just a sightseeing guide to heaven, and it's not our purpose to discuss all the "how to's" of good Christian living. I wish we had more time to talk about the Ten Commandments, the golden rule, the admonition to "judge not, lest you be judged," the power of faith to move mountains, the necessity to "pray always," the need to "take up your cross," the strength to say "not my will, but yours," and the command to "love your neighbor as yourself." These essentials of living a holy life have been beautifully written about in thousands of other books, starting with the Bible itself. It's not my intention here to "sum up" the basics or condense into a short list what really needs to be studied over the course of a lifetime.

But I would like to say one very important thing about getting to heaven, and it has to do with something so basic that it's often overlooked by people who consider themselves believers.

We've said in this book that the best part of heaven will be meeting God—that our relationship with our creator and redeemer is going to be the most fulfilling aspect of our life in paradise. In a real sense, heaven can be defined as "union with God," since that union will give us all the joys that this book has attempted to describe.

Well, if our goal as human beings is to get to heaven, then isn't it obvious what the goal of our lives here on Earth should be?

Our ticket to heaven is the very same thing we are hoping to experience in heaven itself—*union with God*. In fact, not only is that the ticket to heaven, but as we hinted at in the last chapter, it's also the ticket to happiness and fulfillment right now.

Another way of saying all this is that if you want to go to heaven, you must make God the sovereign of your life. God—not some vague spiritual "force," not "mother nature," not the Earth, not some trendy social theory, not money, not power, not fame, not TV, not sex. *God*. The personal God of the Old and New Testaments. The God who asks for your prayers, worship, and obedience. The God who we've spoken about so much in these pages.

The most important thing to reject is the notion that you are your own ticket to heaven. As the saying goes, there are two big lessons to learn in life: There *is* a God; and, I'm *not* him. Sadly, more and more people today are forgetting this. By setting ourselves up as the ultimate arbiters of morality, we, as a society, have thrust ourselves right back into the Garden of Eden, deciding what is right and what is wrong, pretending to be God.

The key to *everything* is that God must be the sovereign of your life. Inviting him into your heart, and then letting that faith infuse every area of your life, is your passport to both earthly and heavenly joy.

Different denominations of believers might have different ways of articulating this truth. A Protestant might describe union with God as accepting Jesus Christ as your personal savior and being born again. A Catholic might urge you to make the Eucharist—the sacrament of the Lord's body and blood—the center of your life. But however you look at it (and I am not trying to downplay the differences between faith traditions) the one unifying belief of all Christians everywhere is that Christ must be lord of your life.[4] Once that happens, then everything else falls into place.

The good news is that it's never too late to get your ticket to heaven. You can even pick it up at the last second—just before you board the plane. When Christ was hanging from the cross, one of the men crucified alongside him said, "Jesus, remember me when you come into your kingdom." That simple profession of faith led Jesus to say, "This very day, you will be with me in paradise." At that moment, a lifelong sinner became a saint. God granted him the gift of heaven, instantaneously, all because he asked for it with faith.[5]

It doesn't matter how old you are or how bad you've been in your life. All the pleasures of heaven are still accessible to you. That's how great God's mercy is.

But isn't this just wishful thinking? Isn't this whole book just wishful thinking? Before we end, I want to say one word about this question—because I don't think there's a more ridiculous argument under the sun than the one that says heaven is just a product of human imagination, based on our desire. To say that religion—particularly Christianity—is wishful thinking flies in the face of all common sense and logic.

Is it wishful thinking to believe in hell, the devil, and demons? Is it wishful thinking to believe we're going to be judged and held accountable for every sin we've ever committed? Is it wishful thinking to believe the best way to live our life is to sacrifice our own desires for the sake of others? Is it wishful thinking to believe that we should discipline our natural bodily urges for the sake of some unseen "kingdom"?

And while we're at it, is it wishful thinking to believe God wants us to *love our enemies?* For goodness sake, what kind of demand is that?

My point is that if human beings were going to invent a religion based on their own wishful thinking, they could do a lot "better" than Christianity. Why in the world would we make things so hard on ourselves? Why not wish for a religion that had a heaven, but at the same time allowed promiscuous sex, encouraged gluttony, did away with all the commandments, and forbade anyone to ever mention the idea of judgment and punishment?

Wouldn't that make a lot more sense?

And yet, there is this notion that heaven is all "fluff" and that we believe in it merely because we're afraid of death and want to see our dead relatives again. Amazing!

The truth is that heaven is not wishful thinking.

Whether or not it makes us feel good is immaterial. If it's not *true*, then I don't want to believe it. If it doesn't exist, I don't want to waste my time on it. The reason why we *can* get so enthusiastic about it is precisely because it's *not* pie in the sky. Christianity as an organized religion is demanding, challenging, provocative, sublime, frustrating at times, and always intellectually stimulating. You can love it, hate it, believe that it's the greatest thing since sliced bread, or the "opiate of the masses," but one thing you can't do is dismiss it as wishful thinking.

People who insist that heaven is just something human beings made up to alleviate grief just don't know much about the process of grieving. No belief—no matter how wonderful—can console you if you've lost someone you love. Those of you who have experienced a *real* loss know what I mean. No one can say anything or do anything to help you. No one understands how you feel. If you've been devastated by someone's death, you are going to have to work, fight, sleep, and live your way through the nightmare. Eventually—and it may take years—the terrible pain in your chest will begin to dull, and finally even subside. Then you'll begin to enjoy life again. But you can be sure there will be many setbacks and bouts of agony along the way.

That's what grieving over the death of someone entails, and I'm afraid nothing—not even heaven—can prevent it from taking its natural course. Do you know how we can be so sure of that? Because Christ himself openly grieved.

Remember the story of the raising of Lazarus?[6] It's one of the most powerful in the Bible. Jesus was off preaching somewhere in Palestine when he was told that his friend Lazarus was dying. When Jesus finally arrived on the scene, Lazarus was already dead and buried and everyone was crying. Lazarus's sisters, Martha and Mary, were especially upset, and Martha sobbed to Jesus, "Lord, if only you had been here, my brother would not have died." Jesus reassured her, "Your brother will rise again." Naturally, Martha didn't understand what he meant, so she just said, "Yes, I know that he will rise again in the resurrection on the last day."

To this, Jesus responded: *I am the resurrection and the life, he that believes in me, even though he dies, will live again. And whoever lives and believes in me will never die.*

They took Jesus to the tomb and he looked around and saw the family of Lazarus grieving. The Gospel of St. John says that he "groaned in the spirit and was troubled." Then we read the shortest sentence in the entire Bible:

"Jesus wept."

Anyone who doesn't think it's okay for people to grieve long and hard should read that again. *Jesus wept.* Here we have God himself crying over the death of someone. The same God who created the world, created human beings, created heaven; who knows heaven exists, not because of "faith," but because of knowledge and personal experience; the same God, moreover, who *knows* that he is about to raise Lazarus from the dead, and that his grieving family is going to be happy again.

And yet he still wept. How can this be?

The reason is that despite his knowledge of heaven, Jesus was upset that everyone was so sad. He was troubled that someone he loved had to die and be locked up in a tomb. He grieved because of the suffering of Lazarus's family. He cried because it was a funeral, and that's what people do at funerals.

In the Gospel account, Jesus goes on to raise Lazarus. All those present are frightened and astounded when the dead man comes out from the tomb, wearing his burial clothes, his face still covered with a shroud. To me, though, the most astonishing thing about the story has always been the lesson it teaches us about God's attitude toward suffering: he allows us to grieve and he allows us to cry, just as he allowed his own son to grieve and cry about Lazarus. Just as he later allowed him to suffer and die on a cross. Even though he knows he's going to make us rise from the dead, and even though he knows he's going to give us the amazing gift of heaven, he hates it when we suffer, and in some special way, suffers right along with us.

One thing that's very obvious is that the Christian teaching on heaven was not concocted to help us get through death and grieving. From the very beginning of the religion, Christians have known that no amount of faith in the afterlife could stop us from crying when someone we love dies.

Once and for all, we believe in heaven because it is true, not because we want it to be true—because it exists, not because we hope it exists.

Now that won't stop people from criticizing us for our beliefs. It won't stop them from saying we are "wasting our time" to be thinking about heaven, and that we are deluding ourselves for not accepting the "reality" of nothingness.

But they can protest all they want. None of it matters. The truth is that heaven really is a paradise, just as we've been taught since we were boys and girls. Nothing we've ever seen compares with it; and all the good times we've experienced in our lives pale next to it. "Eye has not seen, nor ear has heard, what God has prepared for those who love him."[7]

Heaven is a pleasure palace, a fairyland, a nature preserve, a "city, shining on a hill," a great big family reunion, and a never-ending vacation, all rolled into one. It's the ultimate adventure for travelers of all ages, and a place of supreme happiness for the entire human race. And the best news is that after we finish our lives *here*, we can all go *there*—if we choose. How can we be so sure?

Because two thousand years ago, on that first quiet Easter Sunday morning, when it was still dark and everyone was sleeping, Christ *did* rise.

Arrivederci!

Well, we made it! We've traveled to heaven and back.

And that's just the beginning. There's so much I've left out! You know, when you study subjects like biology or history or foreign languages or psychology, you can achieve a certain level of expertise and obtain the title "master." But with theology it's the other way around. You don't ever master that subject, it masters you. If this book has been successful, it *hasn't* answered all your questions. In fact, for every question we've raised, I hope ten more have popped into your head. My greatest desire is that you use this book as a springboard to other, better books about God and heaven.

My focus here has been purposely narrow. I've

avoided speaking about many things that really belong in a book about heaven. For example, I've barely touched on the subject of hell, which is just as important a part of biblical teaching as heaven—and just as physical a place, by the way.[1]

I also haven't mentioned any of the surprises we're going to encounter in the afterlife. Every great trip has surprises. After all, if things went exactly as we planned all the time, traveling wouldn't be much fun. The same holds true for our trip to heaven. Right now we live in a three-dimensional world. We can't imagine what a four- or five-dimensional world will look like. Therefore any description of heaven we come up with is bound to fall short of the mark. It's bound to be too "Earthy."

Unfortunately, there's no way around this. While I believe this book paints a more thorough and realistic picture than many other works that concentrate exclusively on the spiritual characteristics of heaven, I also know that this too is only a feeble attempt to capture something inexpressible—the transcendent imagination of God. Let me say very clearly that when we get to heaven, we are going to be surprised and amazed by a lot of pleasures none of us could ever predict. The joys of heaven will be beyond our wildest dreams.

Whenever I visit a country and have missed out on seeing certain important sights, I tell my wife, "This just means we have to come back." The same is true of these important topics I've either left out or failed to emphasize in this book. We'll just have to revisit them at another time. I didn't want to digress too much in these pages because it's so crucial we understand one, fundamental point. Heaven is the most outrageously happy place we could ever imagine. Any suffering we experience now, no matter how intense, is completely canceled out by the joy that awaits us. It's important that we at least have some idea of *how* that can be—and that's been the simple purpose of this book.

If you don't believe me, or you think I've been exaggerating about the marvels of heaven, I'll tell you what we can do. Instead of arguing, let's just see for ourselves if it's true. Why don't we make a point of getting together—say, one million years from today—and talk about it then? I'm not kidding. Let's all meet in one of heaven's big, wide-open places—like St. Mark's Square in Venice—and talk about this whole subject at length. We can compare notes, laugh about all the silly doubts we had back in our old lives, and then have a big spaghetti meal with some Chianti afterwards.

Is it a date?

Scripture Notes

Since this book was never meant to be a "heavy" academic text, I have not attempted to include an exhaustive list of theological footnotes. Instead, I have provided below a few key scriptural references to back up some of the more important theses contained in these pages.

Flight Plan

1. 1 Chron 16:3; Ps 96:11; Isa 44:23; Mt 13:44; Lk 10:20; 15:7; Heb 12:22; Rev 12:12, 18:20.
2. Rev 7:16–17, 21:4.
3. Jn 14:2–3; 2 Cor 5:1; Dt 26:16; 1 Ki 8:30, 39, 43, 49; 2 Chron 6:21, 30, 33, 39.
4. Rev 4, 5, 7.
5. 2 Cor 5:1; Ps 16:11; Lk 16:9; Jn 3:15–16, 36, 5:24, 6:40, 10:28, 17:3.

Chapter 1

1. Gen 1:1–31, 2:1–25.

2. Jn 14:2–3.

3. Rev 21:1–27.

4. Dt 26:15; 1 Ki 8:30, 39, 43, 49; 2 Chron 6:21, 30, 33, 39, 30:27.

5. 1 Cor 15:20–23, 42–57; 2 Cor 5:1–10; 1 Thess 4:13–18.

6. 2 Pet 3:8.

7. Heb 12:1.

Chapter 2

1. Phil 3:21.

2. Lk 16:23–30.

3. Mt 6:25, 30.

4. Lk 24:13–51; Jn 20:15–22, 24–29, 21:15–22; Acts 1:1–9;
   Mt 28:9, 10, 18.

5. Phil 3:21.

6. Mt 26:41; Mk 14:38.

7. 1 Jn 3:2, 3.

8. Rev 7:16, 17.

Chapter 3

1. Isa 65:17, 66:22; 2 Pet 3:13; Rev 3:12, 21:1, 2.

2. 1 Cor 15:20, 23.

3. Isa 64:4 (cf. 1 Cor 2:9).

4. Rom 8:18–23.

5. Rev 21:1–27.

Chapter 4

1. Gen 2:18.

2. Gen 1:27.

3. Dt 6:4; Mt 28:19; 2 Cor 13:13.

4. Mt 9:18–26; Mk 5:21–42; Lk 8:40–56.

5. 1 Thess 4:13–18; 1 Cor 15:35–57.

6. Gen 1:1; Heb 9:27, 12:23, 13:4; Rom 2:16; 2 Tim 4:1, 8; Jas 4:12; 1 Pet 4:5; 1 Cor 15:50–55.

7. 1 Cor 15:12–19, 32.

8. Mt 22:2, 25:1; Lk 14:15.

Chapter 5

1. Mt 22:30; Mk 12:25; Lk 20:35.

2. Gen 2:18–25; Mt 19:3–7; Mk 10:2–10.

3. Eph 5:21–32.

4. Lk 22:19.

5. Gen 1:28.

6. Jn 13:23, 19:26, 20:2, 21:7, 20.

7. Mt 16:18.

Chapter 6

1. Ps 36:6.

2. Gen 6; Jon 1:17; Lk 2:8; Mt 21:1; Jn 12:12.

3. Mt 3:16; Mk 1:10; Lk 3:22; Jn 1:29, 32, 36.

4. Isa 11:6–8; 65:25.

5. Mt 18:2–4; Mk 10:13–16.

Chapter 7

1. Heb 12:22; Rev 5:11.
2. Rev 12:7.
3. Jude 9; Rev 12:7; Lk 1:19, 26; Tob 3:17.
4. 1 Chron 21:1; Job 1:6, 2:7; Mt 4:10, 16:23; Lk 22:3; 2 Cor 11:14; Rev 12:9, 20:2.
5. Gen 3:24, 22:11; Mt 2:13; Mk 1:13; Lk 1:13, 26–38, 22:43; Rev 8, 9, 15, 16.
6. Mt 18:10.
7. Heb 1:14.
8. Lk 15:10.
9. Col 2:18.

Chapter 8

1. Jn 14:27.
2. Gen 1:1–28.
3. Mk 6:3; Acts 18:3; 2 Thess 11–13.
4. Jn 5:17.

Chapter 9

1. 1 Cor 15:54–57.
2. Rev 21:4; Heb 9:27.

Chapter 10

1. Ex 3:14; Mk 14:62; Jn 8:58, 14:6.
2. Jn 1:1–18.

3. Jn 21:4–15.

4. Jn 16:23.

5. Rom 8:28.

6. 1 Cor 13:12, 13.

7. Rev 5:8, 8:3, 4.

Chapter 11

1. Eph 2:10.

2. Jn 10:10.

3. Mt 3:2, 4:17, 10:7; Lk 21:31.

4. Mt 17:2; Mk 9:2; Lk 9:29.

Chapter 12

1. 2 Cor 4:14–18.

2. Mk 8:36.

3. 1 Cor 15:20–23; Phil 2:8; Rom 5:18–20.

4. Rom 10:9.

5. Lk 23:43.

6. Jn 11:1–56.

7. Isa 64:4; 1 Cor 2:9.

Arrivederci!

1. Mt 5:22, 29, 30, 10:28, 18:9, 23:15, 33; Mk 9:43, 45, 47; Lk 12:5, 16:23; Jas 3:6; 2 Pet 2:4.

Travel Book Bag

On your journey to heaven, here are some great resources to read, enjoy, and study along the way.

Bibles

Holy Bible: New Living Translation. Wheaton, Ill.: Tyndale Publications, 1998.

The Holy Bible: Revised Standard Edition. Catholic Edition. Camden, N.J.: Thomas Nelson & Sons, 1966.

The Holy Bible: King James Version. Illustrated by Barry Moser. New York: Viking Press, 1999.

Other Works

Anderson, Debby. *Let's Talk About Heaven.* Elgin, Ill.: Chariot Books, 1991.

Aquinas, Thomas. *Summa Theologica.* 5 vols. Westminster, Md.: Christian Classics, 1981.

Augustine. *The City of God.* Translated by Marcus Dods. New York: Modern Library, 2000.

Badham, Paul. *Christian Beliefs About Life After Death*. New York: Barnes & Noble Books, 1976.

Blamires, Harry. *Knowing the Truth About Heaven and Hell*. Ann Arbor, Mich.: Servant Books, 1988.

Bondi, Hermann. *Relativity and Common Sense: A New Approach to Einstein*. New York: Dover Publications, 1964.

Bounds, E. M. *Inside Heaven's Gates*. New Kensington, Pa.: Whitaker House, 1985.

Briggs, Constance Victoria. *The Encyclopedia of Angels*. New York: Plume, 1997.

Buddemeyer-Porter, Mary. *Will I See Fido in Heaven? Scripturally Revealing God's Eternal Plan for His Lesser Creatures*. Saint Louis, Mo.: Eden Publications, 1995.

Bullock, Karen O. *The Writings of Justin Martyr*. Nashville, Tenn.: Broadman & Holman, 1998.

Clowes-Johnson, Janet. *Tell Me About Heaven . . . I Think I'm Forgetting*. Nashville, Tenn.: Ideal Children's Books, 1998.

Craig, William Lane. "God, Time, and Eternity." *Religious Studies* 14 (1979): 497–503.

Dravecky, Dave, Jan Dravecky, and Amanda Sorenson. *Glimpses of Heaven, Reflections on Your Eternal Hope*. Grand Rapids, Mich.: Zondervan Publishing House, 1998.

Graham, Billy. *Angels: Ringing Assurance That We Are Not Alone*. Dallas, Tex.: Word Publishing, 1995.

Harris, Murray J. *From Grave to Glory: Resurrection in the New*

Testament. Grand Rapids, Mich.: Zondervan Publishing House, 1990.

Hawking, Stephen. *A Brief History of Time.* Rev. ed. New York: Bantam Books, 1996.

Hopfe, Lewis M. *Religions of the World.* 5th ed. New York: Macmillan, 1991.

Hunt, David. *Whatever Happened to Heaven?* Eugene, Ore.: Harvest House, 1998.

James, John W., and Russell Friedman. *The Grief Recovery Handbook: The Action Program for Moving Beyond Death, Divorce, and Other Losses.* Rev. ed. New York: Harper Perennial, 1998.

Keathley, J. Hampton III. *Angelology: The Doctrine of Angels.* Dallas, Tex.: Biblical Studies Press, 1998.

Kelsey, Morton. *What Is Heaven Like? The Kingdom As Seen in the Beatitudes.* New York: New York City Press, 1997.

Kreeft, Peter. *Heaven.* San Francisco: Ignatius Press, 1989.

———. *Everything You Ever Wanted to Know About Heaven But Never Dreamed of Asking.* San Francisco: Ignatius Press, 1990.

———. *Angels and Demons.* San Francisco: Ignatius Press, 1995.

Kurz, Gary. *Cold Noses at the Pearly Gates.* Kearney, Neb.: Morris Publications, 1997.

Lewis, C. S. *The Discarded Image.* Cambridge: University Press, 1964.

———. *The Great Divorce.* New York: Macmillan, 1946.

———. *The Problem of Pain.* New York: Macmillan, 1962.

———. *Weight of Glory.* Grand Rapids: Eerdmans, 1949.

Lockyer, Herbert. *All the Angels in the Bible.* Peabody, Mass.: Hendrickson, 1996.

Lucas, Daryl J. et al. *104 Questions Children Ask About Heaven and Angels, with Answers from the Bible.* Wheaton, Ill.: Tyndale House Publishers, 1996.

Moody, Raymond A., Jr. *Life After Life.* New York: Bantam Books, 1977.

O'Connor, James T. *Land of the Living.* New York: Catholic Book Publishing, 1992.

Rahner, Karl. *Foundations of Christian Faith.* New York: Seabury Press, 1978.

Ratzinger, Joseph. *Eschatology: Death and Eternal Life.* Washington, D.C.: Catholic University of America, 1988.

Russell, Jeffrey Burton. *A History of Heaven: The Singing Silence.* New Jersey: Princeton University Press, 1997.

Sklar, Lawrence. *Space, Time, and Spacetime.* Berkeley: University of California Press, 1974.

Tada, Joni Eareckson. *Heaven Your Real Home.* Grand Rapids, Mich.: Zondervan Publishing House, 1995.

Van Scott, Miriam. *Encyclopedia of Heaven.* New York: St. Martin's Press, Thomas Dunne Books, 1998.

Acknowledgments

Every time a jet takes off or a ship leaves port, you can be sure that a tremendous amount of teamwork has gone into making the departure successful. So it has been with *A Travel Guide to Heaven.*

My mother and father—Laura and Sal DeStefano—have contributed the most to my life and to the creation of this work. Some of my earliest childhood memories are of my mother talking to me about God and of my father vigorously defending the Faith to family, friends, and strangers. My parents also instilled in me a love for traveling, and an even greater love for reading. My father, in particular, introduced me to a world of art and culture that expanded my horizons in ways I can't begin to measure. Without these influences, I could never have written this book.

Over the years I have been privileged to have some extraordinary teachers. Three who deserve special mention are my kindergarten teacher, Miss Crupi, who gave me a love for school and learning that continues to this day, Frank McCourt, author of *Angela's Ashes*, who taught me much about the craft of writing while I was at Stuyvesant High School, and Dr. Peter Redpath, who gave me a solid grounding in Greek Philosophy, Thomas Aquinas, and critical thinking in general, when I was an undergraduate at St. John's.

The initial idea for this book came to me many years ago after listening to a wonderful homily on heaven preached by Fr. Frank Pavone, national director of Priests for Life. It would be impossible to overestimate what I have learned from Fr. Frank about evangelization, ecumenism, theology, and the Gospel of Jesus Christ. He is a great and brilliant man.

One of the most important groups of people who contributed to this project was my inner circle of trusted readers. My wife, Kimberly, was the first person to see each of the chapters as they were written, and she provided invaluable advice to me on both content and style. Apart from being a gifted teacher, she is also a natural-born editor. My sister Elisa, and my brothers Carmine, Salvatore, and Vito, also read the manuscript as it was being written, and provided me with very helpful feedback.

Lou Aronica, formerly the publisher of Avon books and currently the president of The Fiction Studio, was the first professional to make an editorial pass through the book. His advice proved very useful in producing the final draft. My personal assistants, Tracy Corallo and Jordan Horn, also played a crucial role in the development of the manuscript. I don't know what I'd do without these two incredible ladies.

Perhaps the most challenging aspect of writing this book was trying to make it as acceptable as possible to *all* Christian denominations. To that end, I had a great deal of help from several brilliant scholars and church leaders who read over the finished manuscript and pointed out many passages and phrases that had to be revised, added, or deleted. These scholars included Dr. Michael Crow, Adjunct Professor at Fuller Theological Seminary, Dr. Dick Eastman, International President of Every Home for Christ and the President of the National Prayer Committee, Msgr. Anthony Frontiero, former attaché to Archbishop Renato Martino, the Vatican's delegate to the United Nations, Msgr. George P. Graham (who, along with Bishop William Murphy of the diocese of Rockville Centre, secured an *Imprimatur* for the book), Jeannie Mikkelson, formerly of Bethany House Publishing, Rev. Eric Rapaglia, Rev. Robert Schenck of the Evangelical Church Alliance and President of the National Clergy Council, Dr. Pia de Solenni of the Family Research Council, and lastly, my good friend, Rev. Peter M.J. Stravinskas.

I have been extremely blessed in working with the best editorial staff in the world. The dedicated folks at Doubleday, especially Alexandra Beatty Morris, Judie Jacoby, John Pitts, Jackie Everly, John Fontana, Michael Palgon, Sheila Klee, Marc Winter and Frances O'Connor, have all been wonderful. The president of Doubleday, Steve Rubin, has been marvelously supportive from the beginning, and my editor, Michelle Rapkin, has been an absolute godsend. Her wise, practical, and always gentle advice has been right on target and has contributed immensely to the book. I'm very lucky to have her.

My agent, Peter Miller, from PMA Literary and Film Management, is probably the person most responsible for helping me to get this book published. Of all the agents in New York to whom I sent the manuscript, he was the *only one* who thought it had enough promise to get behind and *push*. I am very grateful to him for his enthusiasm, confidence, and unflagging loyalty.

The greatest thanks, however, must go to my best friend and colleague, Jerry Horn. Jerry, a one-man media/marketing dynamo, researched the publishing world, secured endorsements, handled a thousand logistical details, and performed miracles on demand throughout the entire process. Without him, *A Travel Guide to Heaven* would never have seen the light of day.

Finally, I want to extend my heartfelt gratitude to the hundreds of family members, friends, and acquaintances who have been praying fervently for the book's success for many months.

Thanks again to all of you for making this the best trip of my life!

When Anthony DeStefano wrote *A Travel Guide to Heaven*, he had no idea it would become such a thought-provoking bestseller. His main purpose was to combine rock solid biblical theology with playful speculation and good humor, in order to dare readers to think about their true home — heaven. Utilizing a delightful travel motif, he set out to paint an amazingly vivid picture of the life to come. In doing so, he succeeded in bringing joy, hope, and consolation to people all across the globe. Many have commented on DeStefano's upbeat tone and infectious enthusiasm, but it is undoubtedly his uncanny ability to communicate profound theological ideas in a simple and highly enjoyable way that has captivated and inspired so many readers.

Discussion Questions

1. What has been the most significant change in the way you think about heaven as a result of reading Anthony DeStefano's book?

2. DeStefano writes of the experience of attending fifteen funerals in six months and of being disappointed at times by some of the sermons that were preached on death and the afterlife. Do you think priests, pastors, and other spiritual leaders are doing an effective job at communicating the joyful message of heaven — especially to those who have lost loved ones?

3. Given the Christian teaching that heaven will one day be both physical and spiritual, what do you think it will actually look like?

4. DeStefano movingly describes our first morning in heaven, when we see our loved ones again in bodily form for the first time. Who are you looking forward to seeing most in heaven? What will you say to them?

5. DeStefano says that we will be at our "best" in heaven—physically, mentally, emotionally, spiritually, and psychologically. What kind of person are you when you are at your best? What are the special qualities, personality traits, and gifts that you possess that will add to the life of heaven?

6. According to DeStefano, heaven will be a place filled with energy and activity. What kinds of things do you look forward to doing there?

7. In heaven we will have the opportunity to meet and become friends with people from all different periods in human history. Who are you excited about getting to know?

8. In the chapter entitled *"Do* all dogs go to heaven?" DeStefano takes issue with theologians who argue that

animals are not allowed into paradise. Where do you stand on this question, and have you had any pets that have died that you wish to see again in heaven?

9. Do you think that believing in heaven makes a person more concerned or less concerned about life in this world? Why?

10. Has this book made you think any differently about God? In particular, what do you think is God's attitude towards the physical world, human happiness, pleasure, and suffering?

11. What would your response be to someone who tells you that your belief in heaven is nothing more than "wishful thinking" brought about by a "fear of death"?

12. How, exactly, has our "ticket to heaven" been purchased for us already, and what must we do to actually get to heaven?

About the Author

ANTHONY DESTEFANO has received many prestigious awards from religious communities throughout the world. In 2002, he was given an honorary doctorate from the Joint Academic Commission of the National Clergy Council and the Methodist Episcopal Church for "the advancement of Christian beliefs in modern culture." In 2003, he was made a Knight of the Sovereign Military Order of Malta. Most recently, he was awarded the "Defender of Israel" medal by the Jerusalem Center for Peace Studies. Mr. DeStefano is the CEO of Priests for Life, a Catholic not-for-profit organization based in New York. He is a member of the National Religious Broadcasters Organization (NRB), the Royal Institute of Philosophy in London, and was recently elected a member of the prestigious International Institute for Strategic Studies (IISS), also based in the United Kingdom. An avid pilot, DeStefano serves as a senior member of the U.S. Air Force's auxiliary Civil Air Patrol. He is 40 years old and lives on Long Island with his wife, Kimberly, a kindergarten teacher. *A Travel Guide to Heaven* is his first book.